Series Editor:
Paul Wehman, Ph.D.

Transition to
Adulthood Series

DEMYSTIFYING
Transition
Assessment

The Brookes
Transition to
Adulthood Series

DEMYSTIFYING
Transition
Assessment

by

Colleen A. Thoma, Ph.D.

Department of Special Education and Disability Policy
Virginia Commonwealth University
Richmond

and

Ronald Tamura, Ph.D.

Department of Special Education and Reading
Southern Connecticut State University
New Haven

with invited contributors

·P A U L·H·
BROOKES
PUBLISHING Cᵒ.®

Baltimore • London • Sydney

Paul H. Brookes Publishing Co.
Post Office Box 10624
Baltimore, Maryland 21285-0624
USA

www.brookespublishing.com

Typeset by Scribe, Philadelphia, Pennsylvania.
Manufactured in the United States of America by
Bradford & Bigelow, Newburyport, Massachusetts.

Library of Congress Cataloging-in-Publication Data

Thoma, Colleen A.
  Demystifying transition assessment / by Colleen A. Thoma, Ph.D. and Ronald Tamura, Ph.D.
     pages   cm
  Includes bibliographical references and index.
  ISBN 978-1-59857-214-8 (pbk. : alk. paper)
  ISBN 1-59857-214-8 (pbk. : alk. paper)
1. Youth with disabilities—Education—United States. 2. Youth with disabilities—Employment—United States.
3. People with disabilities—Functional assessment. 4. School-to-work transition—United States. I. Title.

LC4031.T439 2013
371.9—dc23   2012045862

British Library Cataloguing in Publication data are available from the British Library.

2024   2023   2022   2021   2020

10   9   8   7   6   5   4   3   2

Contents

   Ronald Tamura and Colleen A. Thoma

   Transition, Transition Assessment, and IDEA
   Formal Assessments
   Informal Assessments
   Alternative and/or Performance-Based Assessments
   Transition as a Backward Design Process

   Colleen A. Thoma, Roberta Gentry, Kimberly Boyd, and Karren Streagle

   Formal Academic Assessments
   Informal Academic Assessments
   Alternative or Performance-Based Academic Assessments
   Applying the Principles of Universal Design for Learning to Academic Assessment
   Involving Parents in Academic Assessment
   Collaborating with Others in Academic Assessment

   Colleen A. Thoma

   Self-Determination
   Formal Self-Determination Assessments

Colleen A. Thoma and Ronald Tamura

Vision for the Future
Requirements of Postschool Environments
How to Use the Assessment Data to Set Goals
Transition Services and Interagency Linkages
Measuring Progress

Series Preface

The Brookes Transition to Adulthood Series was developed for the purpose of meeting the critical educational needs of students with disabilities who will be moving from school to adulthood. It is no longer acceptable to simply equip a student with a set of isolated life skills that may or may not be relevant to his or her adult life. Nor is it sufficient to treat the student as if he or she will remain unchanged throughout life. As we allow for growth and change in real-life environments, so must we allow for growth and change in the individuals who will operate within the environments. Today, transition must concern itself with the whole life pattern of each student as it relates to his or her future. However, integrating the two constructs of self and the real adult world for one student at a time is not always straightforward. It requires skills and knowledge. It requires a well-thought-out, well-orchestrated team effort. It takes individualization, ingenuity, perseverance, and more.

The results of these first-rate efforts can be seen when they culminate in a student with a disability who exits school prepared to move to his or her life beyond the classroom. Unfortunately, though, this does not always happen. This is because transition has become a splintered concept, too weighted down by process and removed from building on the student's aspirations and desires for "a good life." However, it does not have to be this way.

This book series is designed to help the teachers, transition specialists, rehabilitation counselors, community service providers, administrators, policy makers, other professionals, and families who are looking for useful information on a daily basis by translating the evidence-based transition research into practice. Each volume addresses specific objectives that are related to the all-important and overarching goal of helping students meet the demands of school and society and gain a greater understanding of themselves so that they are equipped for success in the adult world.

Editorial Advisory Board

About the Authors

Colleen A. Thoma, Ph.D., Professor of Special Education and Disability Policy, Virginia Commonwealth University, 1015 W. Main Street, Oliver Hall, Room 4048, Richmond, Virginia 23284

Dr. Thoma earned her doctoral degree from Indiana University and is currently Professor in the Department of Special Education and Disability Policy at Virginia Commonwealth University. Her research interests include preparation of teachers to support self-determined transition planning, student-directed individualized education program development, universal design for transition, postsecondary education transition programs for students with intellectual disability, and the impact of student self-determination on transition and academic outcomes. She currently serves as a member of the Board of Directors for the Council for Exceptional Children, and is a Past President of the Division on Career Development and Transition. She is a recipient of the 2012 Mary E. Switzer Distinguished Research fellowship, conducting a qualitative research study on the education of students with intellectual disability in postsecondary settings. She has authored and coauthored multiple journal articles, book chapters, and conference proceedings related to transition, instructional strategies, and self-determination, including three books: *Transition Assessment: Wise Practices for Quality Lives* (coauthored with Caren L. Sax), *Universal Design for Transition: A Roadmap for Planning and Instruction* (coauthored with Christina C. Bartholomew and LaRon A. Scott), and *Getting the Most Out of IEPs: An Educator's Guide to the Student-Directed Approach*, co-edited with Dr. Paul Wehman.

Ronald Tamura, Ph.D., Associate Professor of Special Education and Reading, Southern Connecticut State University, 501 Crescent Street, Davis 212, New Haven, Connecticut 06515

Dr. Tamura earned his doctoral degree from the University of Nevada, Las Vegas, and is currently Associate Professor at Southern Connecticut State University in the Department of Special Education and Reading where he teaches graduate courses in the areas of developmental disabilities, learning disabilities, collaboration and consultation, and secondary transition. His research interests include personnel preparation, self-determination, transition, and positive behavior supports. He was elected and served as a member of the Board of Directors for the Council for Exceptional Children. He is a former secondary-level special educator and has worked for the Connecticut State Department of Education in the Bureau of Special Education as an Education Consultant. He has contributed as coauthor on journal articles, book chapters, and conference proceedings in the areas of transition, instructional strategies, and self-determination.

About the Contributors

Edwin Achola is an adjunct faculty in the Department of Special Education and Disability Policy at Virginia Commonwealth University. He currently teaches the secondary education and transition planning class designed for practitioners in the M.Ed. program and those seeking special education endorsement. He also teaches an undergraduate special education introductory class. Edwin has worked both as a general and special educator with both high and middle school students in Kenya and the United States. He is also a doctoral student at Virginia Commonwealth University in the same department. Presently, he is engaged in investigating practitioner transition assessment practices and postsecondary education for African American students with intellectual disabilities. His research interests include postsecondary education for students with disabilities, transition planning, and personnel preparation.

Christina C. Bartholomew, Ph.D., is an educational consultant focusing on transition education, student self-determination, collaborative practice, and universal design. She received her Ph.D. in education from Virginia Commonwealth University where she focused her dissertation research on teacher education practices that support student self-determination. She is the coauthor of several book chapters, manuscripts, presentations, and one book, *Universal Design for Transition*, which she coauthored with Colleen A. Thoma and LaRon A. Scott. Her research interests include teacher preparation, self-determination, and universal design for transition.

Elizabeth Battaglia, Ed.D., received her master of science degree in learning disabilities and sixth-year professional diploma in special education from Southern Connecticut State University, New Haven, Connecticut. Dr. Battaglia obtained her doctorate degree in educational instructional leadership K–12 from Argosy University of Sarasota, Florida. Dr. Battaglia is employed by Capital Region Education Council in Hartford, Connecticut. She works around the state to assist school districts with transition planning, assessment, implementation of transition activities, and numerous workshops on transition. Dr. Battaglia is working with several programs to develop 18- to 21-year-old programs for students with disabilities. Her areas of interest include transition assessment, planning effective transition programs for students, developing 18- to

21-year-old programs, differentiation, and infusing vocational skills into the general education curriculum.

Kimberly Boyd, M.T., received her master in teaching degree in special education from Virginia Commonwealth University and is currently a third-year doctoral student in the Department of Special Education and Disability Policy. Her professional areas of interest include working with students with intellectual disability (ID), postsecondary education for students with ID, and the improvement of transition services for all students with disabilities. Ms. Boyd currently works as a special education coordinator for a local public high school.

Lyman L. Dukes, III, Ph.D., is Associate Dean in the College of Education and Associate Professor of Special Education at the University of South Florida St. Petersburg. He has more than 20 years of educational experience. He is co-editor of the book, *Preparing Students with Disabilities for College Success: A Practical Guide to Transition Planning,* and he has published and presented extensively on topics related to postsecondary education and students with disabilities. He has also received transition-relevant grant funding totaling more than $2 million. His current research interests include transition from school to adult life, the Summary of Performance, and the evaluation of postsecondary disability services.

Roberta Gentry, Ph.D., received a bachelor of arts degree in psychology with a minor in sociology from Mary Baldwin College in Virginia. She worked as a neuropsychological test technician and at state and private psychiatric hospitals prior to completing a master of teaching degree at the University of Virginia. She spent almost twenty years in the public school setting as a special education teacher and special education administrator prior to completing her doctoral degree at Virginia Commonwealth University. Currently, Dr. Gentry is Assistant Professor of Special Education at the University of Mary Washington in Virginia.

Joseph W. Madaus, Ph.D., is Director of the Center on Postsecondary Education and Disability and Associate Professor in the Department of Educational Psychology in the Neag School of Education at the University of Connecticut. His research and publication interests include documentation of learning disabilities, transition, assessment, and postschool outcomes of adults with intellectual disabilities.

James E. Martin, Ph.D., is Professor and Zarrow Family Chair in Learning Enrichment at the University of Oklahoma (OU) and is Director of OU's Zarrow Center. Dr. Martin earned his Ph.D. in special education from the University of Illinois in 1983 with a focus on secondary special education and transition. He taught for two years at Eastern Illinois University. He then served as a professor at the University of Colorado at Colorado Springs for 16 years. While at Colorado he served as Special Education Program Coordinator for 10 years and as Director of the Center for Self-Determination. Professor Martin has authored several books, a few dozen chapters for edited books, numerous journal articles, and several curriculum lesson packages, which include video and multimedia applications. He has conducted presentations and training workshops at sites across the United States, Canada, and in Europe. In 2006, CEC's Division on Career Development and Transition awarded Professor Martin the Oliver P. Kolstoe Award for his efforts to improve the quality and access to career and transition services for people with disabilities. His professional interests focus upon the transition of youth with disabilities from high school into postsecondary education and the workforce, and what must be done to facilitate success in high school and postsecondary environments. In particular he examines the application of self-determination methodology to educational and workplace settings.

Mary E. Morningstar, Ph.D., is Associate Professor in the Department of Special Education at the University of Kansas and Director of the Transition Coalition, which offers online transition training and resources for practitioners. She coordinates the online masters program in transition and teaches several classes related to secondary education and transition including vocational training and employment, interagency and community services, and transition assessment. She also coordinates the teacher education program for teachers of students with significant disabilities. Dr. Morningstar has been involved in training and staff development regarding transition from school to adult life for over 25 years. Prior to moving to Kansas, she worked as a teacher for students with significant intellectual disabilities. Dr. Morningstar has been an active advocate for all persons with disabilities based on her experiences as a sibling of a brother with disabilities.

Cynthia Nixon, Ed.D., is currently Associate Professor in Education at Francis Marion University (FMU) in Florence, South Carolina, where she teaches graduate classes in learning disabilities. She received her Ed.D. and M.Ed. from West Virginia University in special education and her undergraduate degree from Fairmont State College in secondary education/U.S. history and geography. She has more than 15 years experience teaching youth with disabilities in West Virginia. Dr. Nixon was Director of Special Education for Richland School District Two and Darlington School District before joining the faculty at FMU. She was also Associate Professor at East Carolina University before moving to South Carolina with her family. She is Past President for the Division on Career Development and Transition (DCDT) and a 25-year member of the Council of Exceptional Children. She is currently the Conference Planner for DCDT. At the state level, Dr. Nixon is a member of the S.C. Transition Advisory Team, treasurer of South Carolina DCDT, and is the National Council for Accreditation of Teacher Education (NCATE) Specialized Professional Association coordinator for the special education program at FMU. She also serves on the Board of Reviewers for NCATE. In addition to her work, Professor Nixon shows and raises Tennessee walking horses.

Karren Streagle, Ph.D., is Assistant Professor of Special Education at Idaho State University, Pocatello, Idaho. She received her Ph.D. in education in special education and disability policy from Virginia Commonwealth University. She has more than 10 years' experience teaching students with mild, moderate, and severe disabilities in self-contained and inclusive settings in Virginia. She served on several state-level standard setting and range finding committees for the Virginia Alternate Assessment Program. She has also taught numerous courses at Virginia Commonwealth University as a collateral and adjunct instructor in the Department of Special Education and Disability Policy and the COVE (Certifying Online Virginia Educators) grant program. Her research interests include alternate and alternative assessments and best practices in academic instruction for students with significant intellectual disabilities.

Preface

Assessment is a critical issue in the implementation of transition planning. Without assessment we cannot determine what and how to teach students as they progress through secondary education to their chosen adult experiences. The following chapters will describe a variety of assessment tools and resources that can be used for planning and implementing steps to achieve individual and family goals for adult life. The assessment process in transition planning is a dynamic experience that can involve many different professionals and service areas, including transition specialists, coordinators, special education teachers, and especially families and the students themselves. Throughout the following chapters the reader will follow an example teacher, Mr. David, as he uses a variety of transition assessment strategies to support two different students on his caseload. We hope that through the use of this transition assessment resource as a part of *The Brookes Transition to Adulthood Series,* students with disabilities will have a smooth, effective, and efficient transition to their own individual goals in adulthood.

Chapter 1 provides the reader with an overview of the transition assessment process as defined in the Individuals with Disabilities Education Improvement Act (IDEA) of 2004 (PL 108-446). The reader is introduced to Mr. David and two of the students that will be on his caseload throughout the book. We learn about the importance for transition assessment and the transition process through Mr. David's use of the assessment process with students with varying support needs.

Chapter 2 provides information related to academic assessment and how it connects to transition assessment to support college and career-focused goals. Issues related to the Common Core State Standards and No Child Left Behind are presented in this chapter as Mr. David proceeds through the transition process with his students.

The importance of self-determination in transition assessment is presented in Chapter 3. Links between self-determination and transition planning have been shown to improve outcomes in several areas. Professionals will learn how to conduct self-determination assessments to improve levels of self-determination and inform the transition process.

Chapter 4 takes a look at the area of employment assessment. Mr. David uses both formal and informal employment interest inventories and surveys to determine the needs and preferences of his students for the world of work. Employment assessment options are from a variety of nontraditional educational sources and these resources are discussed in this chapter.

For some students with disabilities, postsecondary education is considered as an option during transition planning. However, with creative and innovative assessment strategies more students can achieve the goal of postsecondary education. With the consideration of specific goals and supports needed, Chapter 5 describes assessments used for postsecondary education.

Chapter 6 describes assessments related to health and wellness for students transitioning from pediatric, child-centered services to adult health care options. Various assessments and strategies are described that look at health care needs, both immediate and long term, as well as employment options that may be more likely to provide health, disability and life insurance.

Community assessment is explored in Chapter 7 as Mr. David explores a difficult area in conducting transition assessments. The community agencies and resources available to an individual in his or her area must not only be assessed related to the student's needs, but additional assessment and collaboration must be established with community resources as well.

Chapter 8 will review all of the assessment areas and Mr. David's progress in transition planning with his students as they move through the transition process toward adulthood. This chapter also includes a look at the "big picture" of transition planning, such as looking at future visions and planning processes for the students and their family.

In closing, this book will serve as a valuable resource for transition assessment and planning for students' futures. It will be useful for a wide range of stakeholders in the transition process including transition specialists, coordinators, secondary high school special educators, families, and students with disabilities.

REFERENCE

Individuals with Disabilities Education Improvement Act (IDEA) of 2004, PL 108-446, 20 U.S.C. §§ 1400 *et seq.*

Acknowledgments

We are so excited to be part of *The Brookes Transition to Adulthood Series*, and in particular to have had the opportunity to work on this book on transition assessment, the starting point for the development and implementation of successful transition practice.

Our approach to writing this book was to provide a wide range of assessment tools to be used in the transition planning process for stakeholders in the transition process, including transition specialists, coordinators, secondary high school special educators, families, and students with disabilities. We wanted to both provide a comprehensive overview of the process, as well as provide concrete examples. Throughout the chapters of this book, we track the practices employed by a transition specialist, "Mr. David," as he learns about transition assessment and applies what he learns to meet the needs of two students, Chris and Michelle. Of course, the examples provide only one example of how the information included in this book can be used to meet the transition assessment needs of your students.

No doubt you have heard the saying that "it takes a village"; well, we certainly have learned that it takes a village to write a book. We would like to thank those individuals who helped support us throughout this process. First, we would like to express our heartfelt appreciation to Rebecca Lazo, Senior Acquisitions Editor at Paul H. Brookes Publishing Co., for her tireless dedication to this project and ongoing support. Rebecca shares our love for transition and she is a thoughtful, responsive editor of our work. We would also like to thank Stephen J. Plocher, Associate Editor for Paul H. Brookes Publishing Co., for his own guidance and support on this project, as well as Lynda Phung and Caitlyn Ahern and the rest of the Paul H. Brookes production and marketing teams. We would like to acknowledge the series editor, Paul Wehman, and the Editorial Board members, Renee Cameto, Teresa Grossi, Debra Hart, Peg Lamb, David Test, Barbara Guy, Richard Rosenberg, and Mike Wehmeyer for their support of this project. Their leadership in developing a series of practical, evidence-based books to guide the practice of transition stakeholders is a model of collaboration for the field.

We would like to acknowledge our chapter contributors, Edwin Achola, Christina C. Bartholomew, Elizabeth Battaglia, Kimberly S. Boyd, Lyman Dukes, III, Roberta Gentry, James Martin, Joseph Madaus, Mary Morningstar, Cynthia Nixon, and Karren Streagle, for their time and willingness to share their expertise to this project. Some of these contributors were asked to step in at the eleventh hour and we appreciate their work and dedication to the field. Your contributions made the book even better than we initially imagined it would be.

Next, we would like thank our families, Mike and Chris Thoma, and Judy Terpstra, Jackson, Sara, and Kylie Tamura for their support and patience throughout this project. It was a tough year for all of us as we worked on the book, and they gave us the strength to persevere in meeting this goal despite illness, overextended schedules, and an unexpected and devastating family tragedy for Colleen. "Mr. David" was modeled after her beloved brother who passed away in December. Although he was not an educator, he taught her much about life and caring for others. His ability to see the joy in life and to identify what is really important is an important lesson for all of us as we help students make plans for their future and envision their adult lives.

Finally, we would like to acknowledge all the transition specialists, coordinators, secondary high school special educators, and families of students with disabilities who search for appropriate assessment tools to help guide their work to facilitate successful transitions for students. It is not an easy task, but it is the critically important first step. We acknowledge that you are the reason we have to keep moving forward; to help youth with disabilities find a path to meet their goals for adult life.

To the transition specialists, coordinators, and secondary high school special educators who make a difference in the lives of youth with disabilities as they plan for life after high school. You inspire us with your dedication to helping youth imagine a life full of possibilities, identifying the steps and supports needed to get there, and ultimately transitioning to a preferred adult lifestyle. We hope this book will provide additional resources you can use to make the daily challenges manageable and student goals attainable.

1

Transition Assessment

Ronald Tamura and Colleen A. Thoma

What do you want to do after high school? Many teenagers struggle with answering that question and often will answer it by saying that they don't know. While some students know exactly what they want to do and where they want to live—and with whom—many articulate more vague ideas or have tentative plans that change as experience and life events shift. But even the students who answer by saying "I don't know" generally have ideas about some of the components of their vision for an adult life. For example, they might plan to go to college after high school but might not have a specific employment goal. Students this age typically need help learning about their options and envisioning a full life that includes goals in multiple life domains, as Figure 1.1 illustrates.

This book will help guide you to use assessments to help students with disabilities identify their plans for adult life and to establish the steps that will help them achieve those goals. It is an exciting and challenging process of discovery—one in which the assessments themselves can become part of the learning experience. Sitlington, Neubert, and Clark define *transition assessment* as "an ongoing and coordinated process that begins in the middle school years and continues until students with disabilities graduate or exit the school system. Transition assessment assists students with disabilities and their families to identify and plan for postsecondary goals and adult roles" (2010, p. 1).

It is a process for determining a student's strengths, preferences, and interests, which are then used to identify appropriate instruction, supports, and services that assist in the transition from school to postschool life. It is a discovery process that, if done well, illuminates a path for his or her future. And that's what transition assessment is all about: identifying activities that help students and their transition planning team learn more about themselves so they can make "wise decisions" (Thoma, Bartholomew, & Scott, 2009, p. 13) for their adult lives.

This book follows Mr. David, a transition specialist who works for a school district in a state in the Midwest, as he learns about transition assessment and applies what he learns in order to meet the needs of the students he is responsible to assess. In particular, the book will chronicle the assessment strategies he found useful in assessing two students, Chris and Michelle, who illustrate the range of assessment needs.

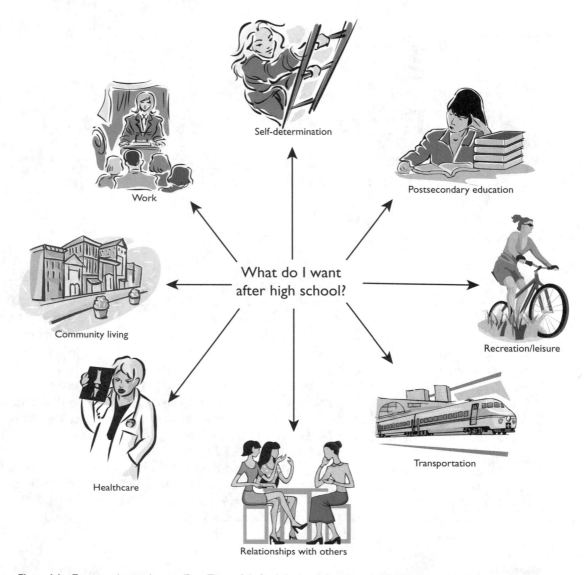

Self-determination

Work

Community living

Healthcare

What do I want
after high school?

Postsecondary education

Recreation/leisure

Transportation

Relationships with others

Figure 1.1.   Transition planning domains. (From Thoma, C.A., Bartholomew, C.C., & Scott, L.A. [2009]. *Universal design for transition: A roadmap for planning and instruction* [p. 12]. Baltimore, MD: Paul H. Brookes Publishing Co.; adapted by permission.)

MEET MR. DAVID AND TWO STUDENTS

Mr. David

Mr. David is in his first year of his position as a transition specialist for a small school district in the Midwest. He is excited about this position since he has recently completed a graduate degree program in transition, and he's looking forward to applying that knowledge in the real world. Mr. David has had less direct experience than most of the other teachers in his graduate program since his previous teaching job was in a middle school and he was responsible for the education of students younger than 14. But he always saw the need to begin transition planning early, and he found ways to link academic instruction to real-world skills and events so as to increase students' interest in learning the material and create an opportunity to prepare them, ultimately, for their adult lives; in fact, that was what drew him to enroll in the graduate program. In addition, Mr. David himself struggled in the transition from high school to adult life and in finding his own vision for an adult life. He wants to mentor others and help them make informed decisions.

Mr. David is responsible for a relatively diverse group of students who attend two different high schools in the area. These students have a wide range of support needs and represent each of the disability categories recognized by the school district and Individuals with Disabilities Education Improvement Act (IDEA) of 2004 (PL 108-446). This book highlights two of these students, Michelle and Chris, who represent students with very different strengths and needs related to transition assessment. Michelle, as a young woman with autism, requires that transition assessment be conducted creatively and collaboratively, since she is not always able to communicate her preferences and interests verbally. Chris, as a young man with attention-deficit/hyperactivity disorder (ADHD), is the type of student for whom transition planning and services is often overlooked, since he is on target to graduate from high school on time and with a standard diploma and to transition to college and employment. While each of these students has different needs that will require different transition assessment practices, they each need a focused and coordinated transition assessment process nonetheless. The following information describes each of these students.

Michelle

Michelle is a 16-year-old with autism who sporadically uses a communication device to interact with others around her. She is currently a sophomore in high school and is included in the general education classes for English, science, math, world history, physical education, and art. She also attends a resource room setting for one period a day during which time she receives extra help learning study skills, transition, and other individualized education program (IEP) goals. On most days, her behavior gets in the way of her learning, but her school fully includes all students in general education classrooms, providing necessary supports wherever the student is.

Michelle is a friendly person who likes to listen to music and spend time with her small group of friends. Michelle gets help from her parents to complete most daily activities, although her teachers believe she could and should do more of these independently. Michelle seems to like her world history class the best, as she seldom engages in disruptive behavior in that class. Her world history teacher often has the students in the class interact as part of her "living history" curriculum. Michelle really liked when she was able to dress like a Roman when learning about Rome and the influence that Rome had on the world.

Michelle's disruptive behaviors include hitting her own face, making loud noises, and walking or running around the classroom. Such behaviors seem to occur when Michelle is asked to focus on work quietly at her desk or when the work is particularly difficult. A functional behavior analysis confirmed that the behaviors function to provide an opportunity for her to escape or avoid an unpleasant or difficult situation. Her teacher has been working to help her learn one or two replacement behaviors to either 1) ask for help or 2) request a break, but she has experienced limited success.

Michelle rides the bus to and from school every day, and she also has an older brother who also attends the same high school. When asked about the future, Michelle doesn't indicate any interest in either working or going to college. Her parents have asked Mr. David to help them with transition planning, but he has struggled with finding a way to understand what Michelle might want to do in the future.

Mr. David is considering recommending that Michelle start the school's vocational program, which would allow her to receive credit for work experience in lieu of her resource period. Due to Michelle's challenging behavior, the teacher of the vocational courses is hesitant to accept her into the program, but Mr. David believes that if they could find a job that Michelle would enjoy, she would do well. The vocational program that the school offers includes a variety of work experiences (e.g., office, daycare, nurse's office, library, auto shop, wood shop, and a variety of off-campus sites). Some of the off-campus sites include the local hospital, a large retail store, a lawyer's office, a fast food restaurant, and a catering business. The vocational program also includes an off-campus apartment that can be used to teach skills that students might need to learn in order to live more independently.

Chris

Chris is a 16-year-old who has been identified as having ADHD. Chris is currently a sophomore in high school who is in general education classes, including English, honors chemistry, honors geometry, world history, Spanish, physical education, and jazz band.

Chris would be considered to be nervous or uncertain at times when interacting with adults; however, he likes to engage his peers in conversations about music and girls. Chris has been playing the guitar since he was 12 years old and has developed into a gifted player who frequently plays in concerts at the school and also has started his own band (as the lead guitarist). Chris would say that he likes school but finds a lot of the material and lessons boring. He especially loves his honors chemistry class because he is allowed to create different compounds and work with his hands. He generally does well in class, but at times he forgets to complete homework or turn it in on time. He struggles with organizing his work, his time, and his materials in general.

He would also say that he likes hanging out at the lake with his friends and eating pizza. Chris is learning how to drive, making his parents nervous about his distractibility and lack of focus. He takes the bus to and from school but cannot wait until he can drive to school. When asked about the future, Chris would say, "I know that my parents want me to go to college, but I would like to travel around Europe for a year and just relax. I would like to go to college for computer science eventually." Finishing high school cannot come soon enough for Chris.

This year, Chris is meeting with his counselors to discuss future college options, and he will be setting up various campus visits for the summer with his parents. He will also be thinking about taking more science and math courses at the honors level during his junior year. He has said that if he goes to college, he would like to live in an apartment or a dorm but is not sure where he would like to go.

Now that the transition specialist, Mr. David, and two students, Chris and Michelle, have been introduced, this chapter will provide an overview of transition assessment strategies.

TRANSITION, TRANSITION ASSESSMENT, AND IDEA

IDEA 2004 (PL 108-446) defines transition services as

> a coordinated set of activities for a child with a disability that is designed to be within a results-oriented process, that is focused on improving the academic and functional

achievement of the child with a disability to facilitate the child's movement from school to post-school activities including post-secondary education, vocational education, integrated employment (including supported employment), continuing and adult education, adult services, independent living, or community participation; it is based on the individual child's needs, taking into account the child's strengths, preferences, and interests; and includes instruction, related services, community experiences, the development of employment and other post-school adult living skills and functional vocational evaluation. (§ 1401[602][34])

This definition highlights the main purpose of transition assessment: that is, identifying a student's postschool goals as well as his or her strengths, preferences, and interests. Not only is transition assessment a wise practice; it is also a required part of a student's education plan. IDEA 2004 requires that the individualized education program (IEP) for students age 16 years or older must include "appropriate measurable postsecondary goals based on age-appropriate transition assessments related to training, education, employment, and, where appropriate, independent living skills" (Title 34, C.F.R. 300.320[b] and [c]; Title 20, U.S.C. § 1414[d][1][A][i][VIII]).

In order to create and implement measurable postsecondary education goals, you must understand what information is needed to create a full picture of a student's strengths, needs, preferences, and interests; make informed decisions about which types of assessments would yield that information; and, once the types are identified, feel confident that you are choosing specific assessments that would determine how you can use that information gathered through assessments (e.g., formal, informal, alternative/performance based) in order to develop transition planning.

Wiggins and McTighe (2006) recommend a backward design process to help teachers effectively link instruction and assessment. This approach uses three steps, which are outlined in Table 1.1.

Purposes of Transition Planning

Consider the wide range of students in order to understand the possible purposes for assessment that would need to be included in a comprehensive transition assessment

Table 1.1. Backward design process applied to transition assessment

Step	Definition	Transition example
Identify desired results	Determine what you want students to know, understand, and/or be able to do.	What do you want to understand about a student's preferences, interests, strengths, and/or needs? Do you want to assess one transition domain such as employment or a more global area such as self-determination? What are the student's goals for his or her own transition to adult life?
Determine acceptable evidence	What type of information will provide evidence of a student's strengths and needs and/or preferences and interests?	What type of assessment data will you need? Will you need performance-based information, or will a more formal assessment be necessary? How will you know whether a student's goals are attainable?
Plan learning experiences	What types of learning experiences or other instructional activities will be needed to meet the desired results?	What transition experiences do you need to provide students so that they can achieve their transition outcomes?

Source: Wiggins and McTighe (2006).

process. First, and most obvious, is the need to assess student preferences and interests across the range of transition domains. Those assessments are needed to provide a *vision* for the student's adult life in terms of employment, postsecondary education, community living, independence, transportation, and recreation/leisure activities. This vision serves as the beginning of the backward planning process: Before a transition plan can be put in place, the desired outcome (or result) needs to be identified.

Educators who work with students with disabilities from culturally and linguistically diverse backgrounds need to use assessment strategies that match the same purposes as assessment strategies of students with disabilities, but they may need to use modified strategies to ensure that the assessments are culturally sensitive and/or translated into the student's native language when necessary. Trainor indicated that research is needed to determine whether current transition assessment and educational practices are effective "in addressing the specific strengths and needs of diverse youth with disabilities due to a lack of empirical investigations that have taken participants' sociocultural backgrounds into consideration" (2008, p. 153). Tips and strategies for conducting an appropriate transition assessment for students from culturally and linguistically diverse backgrounds are included throughout this book, but educators who work with this unique population of students should seek more detailed information from books and guides specifically focused on this topic (see Greene, 2011).

The second purpose of transition assessment is to determine *student strengths and needs* that relate to making that vision a reality. Mr. David needs information that could be used to identify annual goals and the supports, services, and accommodations that a specific student would need to achieve that vision for an adult life. This part of transition assessment should provide information about the requirements of the postschool settings so that it can be determined whether a student has the necessary skills to succeed in that new environment. And in those instances when the student does not have the requisite skills, the transition plan can articulate the coordinated set of activities that will help him or her realize that vision for the future. This purpose of transition assessment would include an assessment of self-determination, aptitude, and achievement and functional skills. It includes a baseline assessment as well as an assessment of progress on meeting annual and long-range transition goals.

The third and final purpose of transition assessment is to *document eligibility* for the various adult services a student would need in order to make his or her vision for an adult life a reality. This might include the information necessary to document one's disability to receive services at college for Chris or the application for vocational rehabilitation services for Michelle. For other students, it might include a reevaluation for Social Security Disability Insurance (SSDI) or an application for Section 8 housing assistance. Applying for these kinds of adult services generally is not the responsibility of transition specialists like Mr. David, but such specialists do play a role in helping students and parents become

Did You Know?

A person-centered planning process can be used to meet the first purpose of transition assessment, helping culturally and linguistically diverse (CLD) students with disabilities and their families "actively participate in the planning for the future and identify cultural, economic and community variables that may impact transition planning" (Neubert, 2012, p. 83).

aware of the different types of services that might be available, providing contact information and inviting representatives of these agencies to participate in transition planning meetings, and/or providing educational documentation to support an eligibility determination when requested by the student and family. This purpose for transition assessment also includes completing a Summary of Performance (SOP): a document that provides a description of the results of assessments completed throughout a student's academic career as well as the services provided to that student while in school. The SOP is defined by IDEA 2004 as "a summary of the child's academic achievement and functional performance, which shall include recommendations on how to assist the child in meeting the child's postsecondary goals" (§ 300.305[e][3]).

Assessment as a Process of Discovery

To better understand effective transition assessment strategies, it is important to start by identifying effective assessment strategies in general. While some assessment resources categorize assessment practices into two broad categories—formal and informal (e.g., Spinelli, 2012; Test, 2012)—it can be even more helpful to categorize assessment practices into three distinct groups: formal, informal, and alternative/performance-based (Thoma et al., 2009). That distinction can help educational professionals think broadly about the range of assessment procedures and include the kinds of performance-based assessments that are particularly useful in terms of informing transition planning. Three categories or types of assessments make a distinction between informal and paper-and-pencil types of assessments and those that require a student to perform some activity to demonstrate his or her knowledge and/or skill. The following sections will explore each of these three types of assessment procedures and their application to transition planning.

Mr. David reviewed the characteristics of each of the three types of assessments—and examples of specific assessment strategies that fall under each—to help him begin to identify transition assessment strategies and instruments that he could use for Chris and Michelle. A list of transition assessments is included at the end of this book. This transition assessment list includes a range of assessments that are available for purchase or at no cost, cover one or more transition planning areas, and fall into one or more assessment categories. This list is meant to be as comprehensive as possible, but it is important to note that given individual student's unique needs, there may be other available assessment procedures not listed that might be more appropriate.

FORMAL ASSESSMENTS

Formal assessments, or standardized assessments, "compare a student's performance with that of peers who are similar in age or grade level" (Spinelli, 2012, p. 57). Formal

---

Did You Know?

The word *assessment* comes from the Latin word *assidere*, which means "to sit down to" (Wiktionary, 2012). Remember to be sure that your transition assessment process honors this spirit; in addition to the formal assessment procedures you use, ensure that you honor what you know about students from the time you spend with them.

Cultural and Linguistic Diversity Tip
When trying to identify a formal assessment for use with students from diverse cultural and/or linguistic backgrounds, pay attention to information about its reliability and validity for those specific subpopulations. If available, this information can be found in the reviews published in the *Mental Measurements Yearbook* as well as in the instructional manuals provided with each formal assessment.

assessments are objective tests developed by experts and designed to be administered to a large group of individuals. These assessments are administered, scored, and interpreted according to specific standards. Formal assessments are developed to be used by a specific group of individuals (by age or other categorization such as disability, ethnic background, or language–to name a few), to be reliable, and to be valid. Before choosing a formal assessment, Mr. David reviewed this information in the technical manual to determine 1) whether the test was designed for use with students like Chris or Michelle, 2) what it was designed to measure (validity), and 3) how consistently it measured what it was designed to measure (reliability). This information will help meet the second step of the backward design process; that is, it will help answer the question of whether the assessment provides acceptable evidence to determine whether desired results are achieved.

Formal assessments can be designed to measure what someone has already learned (achievement) or what he or she might be capable of learning in the future (aptitude); they may be part of a standardized vocational evaluation; or they can be used to categorize an individual student into a specific subgroup based on disability, personality, or level of a specific characteristic such as self-determination. In the realm of transition planning, a number of formal assessments have been used to help guide the process. Achievement tests can assess

- Academic achievement, such as the Woodcock-Johnson III NU Tests of Achievement (Woodcock, McGrew, & Mather, 2007) or the ACT test for college admission (ACT, 2007)

- Adaptive behavior, such as the Vineland Adaptive Behavior Scales, Second Edition (Sparrow, Cicchetti, & Balla, 2005)

- Work performance measures, such as the Job Observation and Behavior Scale (Rosenburg & Brady, 2000)

Achievement tests that measure academic skills can include the Kaufman Test of Educational Achievement–Second Edition (KTEA-2; Kaufman & Kaufman, 2004) or the Peabody Individual Achievement Test–Revised–Normative Update (PIAT-R/NU; Markwardt, 1997). These types of assessments are used to gather individual student information related to an academic area such as writing.

Aptitude tests can assess the potential to perform academic or other work. They compare how a student's performance on an assessment compares to a normed group that has been successful in the setting or in meeting work expectations. For example, Chris's performance on the Scholastic Aptitude Test (SAT) would be compared to the SAT performance of other students who were successful in academic study at the postsecondary level. These tests are predictors of achievement rather than actual measures of ability. Aptitude tests can assess academic potential, such as success in taking the SAT tests, or general or specific work behaviors, such as the following:

- General work aptitude, as assessed by the Occupational Aptitude Survey and Interest Schedule (Parker, 2002) and the Armed Services Vocational Aptitude Battery (U.S. Military Entrance Processing Command, 2005)

- Specific work aptitude, as assessed by the Bennett Mechanical Comprehension Test (Bennett, 2006)

- Potential to adjust to work environments, as assessed by Becker's Work Adjustment Profile (Becker, 2000) or the Work Personality Profile (Bolton & Roessler, 2008)

- Match between personality and work environments, as assessed by the Myers-Briggs Type Indicator (Myers & McCaulley, 1985)

- Match between interests and job requirements, as assessed by the Harrington-O'Shea Career Decision-Making System (Harrington & O'Shea, 2000) and the Wide Range Interest and Occupation Test (Glutting & Wilkinson, 2003)

Adaptive behavior and independent living assessments measure the level and amount of support needed and can include the Brigance Life Skills Inventory (Brigance, 1994) or the Vineland Adaptive Behavior Scales–Second Edition (Vineland II; Sparrow, Cicchetti, & Balla, 2005). These types of assessments would be used to identify any support needs for a particular student in the area of community participation.

Aptitude tests also measure specific abilities, usually in certain vocational areas, and can include the Armed Services Vocational Aptitude Battery (ASVAB; U.S. Military Entrance Processing Command, 2005) or the Occupational Aptitude Survey and Interest Schedule–Third Edition (OASIS-3; Parker, 2002). These assessments can be used to identify areas where a student would be successful in postsecondary education or employment.

Interest inventories measure interests relative to occupational areas and can include the Becker Reading Free Interest Inventory–Revised (Becker, 2000) or the Wide Range Interest-Opinion Test–Revised (WRIOT-R; Glutting & Wilkinson, 2003). A student would take these types of assessments to identify what he or she likes or dislikes as related to a variety of activities or jobs.

Self-determination measures examine a number of component skills (e.g., problem solving, choice making, self-advocacy) and can include the American Institutes for Research (AIR) Self-Determination Scale (Wolman, Campeau, DuBois, Mithaug, & Stolarski, 1994) or the ARC's Self-Determination Scale (Wehmeyer & Kelchner, 1995). These scales do just what their names imply by gathering information regarding a student's level of self-determination.

Resources for Formal Assessments

As stated previously, formal standardized assessments are evaluated based on their reliability, validity, suitability, and objectivity. A number of online resources are available for learning about specific standardized assessment instruments that could be used to match a specific purpose for assessment with a list of possible formal assessment options. The *Mental Measurement's Yearbook* is one such resource that can be accessed through a library's reference section or online through the publisher, Buros, at http://buros.unl.edu/buros/jsp/search.jsp. The *Mental Measurement's Yearbook* provides a listing of formal assessments, including the publisher and a review of each assessment (purpose, reliability, validity, and expert analysis of the tests' strengths and weaknesses); it does not provide the actual assessment instrument itself. Another online resource that provides information specifically about transition assessment instruments is a manual from the Connecticut Department of Education (http://ctserc.org/transition/transition_assessment.pdf).

INFORMAL ASSESSMENTS

Informal assessments could be curriculum based and are sometimes teacher made. They help to identify areas of strengths and areas of need and include a number of different formats.

Interviews and questionnaires help one understand preferences and interests and can include the Dream Sheet (Test, Aspel, & Everson, 2006) and the Enderle-Severson Transition Rating Scales–Third Edition (Enderle & Severson, 2003). Mr. David could gather important information about Michelle or Chris related to their preferences and interests. See Figure 1.2 for a copy of the Dream Sheet.

Direct observation is a method used to observe a specific student in a particular setting, such as a job site, classroom, or community. The information about student performance can then be used to identify areas of strengths and areas of need. Observations can be recorded as a narrative of the activities that take place in the setting during the time frame or can be set up as a checklist of specific behaviors that may or may not occur. With a checklist, observers can decide if they want to indicate whether the specific behaviors were observed, or they can record the frequency and/or intensity of the behavior.

Environmental and situational analysis is a method that can be used to take a closer look at the environment or situation in which a student will be learning or working and determine whether any modifications and/or accommodations to the environment or situation are necessary to support the success of the individual.

Curriculum-based assessments provide a way to determine student performance in reference to a specific curriculum. This information is then used to construct lessons that are specific to an individual student's strengths and needs. Examples of curriculum-based measures that provide information related to transition planning include the Brigance Transition Skills Inventory (Curriculum Associates, 2010) and the Life Centered Education (LCE; CEC, 2012) Transition Curriculum.

Transitional planning inventories assess skills needed to transition from school to the community. The information collected from these assessments can be used to plan for postsecondary education, employment, independent living, and community living, and the measures could include the Transition Planning Inventory–Second Edition (Patton & Clark, in press) or the TEACCH Transition Assessment Profile–Second Edition (Mesibov, Thomas, Chapman, & Schopler, 2007). While transition planning inventories and interest inventories are good starting points for transition assessment, the results are dependent on the degree to which a student knows his or her preferences. The more limited the experiences of students, the less valid the results tend to be; therefore, when dealing with students with disabilities who have fewer experiences, it is important that the information collected from these types of assessment be further validated through an in vivo assessment process.

There are obviously a number of informal assessment procedures that can inform transition planning, but how does a teacher or transition coordinator decide which ones to choose? A model proposed by Hughes and Carter (2002; 2012) to identify the purpose

Student Dream Sheet

Student Name: _____   Initial Date: _____
School: _____   Teacher: _____

Review Dates: _____   _____
              _____   _____

Anticipated Date of Graduation: _____

The following questions will be used to assist in transition planning activities and to determine post school goals.

1. Where do you want to live after graduation?
   _____
   _____

2. How do you intend to continue learning after graduation?
   _____
   _____

   What types of things do you want to learn after graduation?
   _____
   _____

   Where do you want this learning to occur?
   _____
   _____

3. What kind of job do you want now?
   _____
   _____

4. What kind of job do you want when you graduate?
   _____
   _____

(continued)

Figure 1.2. Student Dream Sheet.

From Test, D.W., Aspel, N.P., & Everson, J.M. (2006). *Transition methods for youth with disabilities* (p. 75). Upper Saddle River, NJ: Pearson Merrill Prentice Hall. Reprinted by permission of N.P. Aspel. In *Demystifying Transition Assessment* by Colleen A. Thoma, Ph.D., and Ronald Tamura, Ph.D. (2013, Paul H. Brookes Publishing Co., Inc.)

Student Dream Sheet *(continued)*

5. Where do you want to work?

_____

_____

6. What type of work schedule do you want?

_____

_____

7. What type of pay and benefits do you want from your future job?

_____

_____

8. Do you have any significant medical problems that need to be considered when determining post school goals?

_____

_____

9. What type of chores do you do at home?

_____

_____

10. What equipment / tools can you use?

_____

_____

11. What choices do you make now?

_____

_____

12. What choices are made for you that you want to take charge of?

_____

_____

13. What type of transportation will you use after you graduate?

_____

_____

14. What do you do for fun now?

_____

_____

15. What would you like to do for fun in the future?

_____

_____

From Test, D.W., Aspel, N.P., and Everson, J.M. (2006). *Transition methods for youth with disabilities* (p. 75). Upper Saddle River, NJ: Pearson Merrill Prentice Hall; reprinted by permission of N.P. Aspel. In *Demystifying Transition Assessment* by Colleen A. Thoma, Ph.D., and Ronald Tamura, Ph.D. (2013, Paul H. Brookes Publishing Co., Inc.)

of informal transition assessments can help narrow down the choices by focusing on the purposes of the assessment and using that information to identify assessment strategies that address those purposes. Although originally designed to identify informal and alternative/performance-based assessments, these eight steps could also guide the model for the entire transition assessment process. See Figure 1.3 for the transition assessment model, which uses eight steps to plan transition goals and objectives.

To determine the purpose of the assessment, it is important to know the outcome desired. And of course, by remembering that transition planning is a backward planning/design process, one in which the outcome or end result is identified first, transition coordinators and special educators can ensure that the steps necessary to help the student achieve his or her desired adult outcomes are identified.

ALTERNATIVE AND/OR PERFORMANCE-BASED ASSESSMENTS

Alternative and/or performance-based assessments, sometimes defined as informal assessments, involve students demonstrating and/or developing a portfolio or other collection of their work. These assessments, like the other informal assessments already mentioned, are more subjective than formal assessments since they do not involve a set procedure for administering or evaluating the results. However, for the purposes of transition planning, they provide information about a student's ability to perform the required components of a postschool goal such as employment or taking a bus to get to the college campus. While these assessments can yield critically important information, incorporating alternative and/or performance-based assessments requires planning to ensure that these assessments are more than an overwhelming, random collection of information. Performance-based assessments should be clearly focused (remember the purpose of the assessment) and organized in such a way as to provide a picture of student abilities and demonstrate growth over time. In addition to being focused and organized, good performance-based assessments are *authentic*—that is, they require that students "use knowledge in real-world ways, with genuine purposes, audiences, and situational variables" (Wiggins & McTighe, 2006, p. 337). In addition, it is important to note that these "assessments . . . should teach students (and teachers) what the 'doing' of a subject looks like and what kinds of performance challenges are actually considered most important" (Wiggins & McTighe, 2006, p. 337).

Portfolios are collections of student work that, when viewed together, provide a broad view of a student's achievement (Wiggins & McTighe, 2006). The artifacts in a portfolio can include samples of student work; copies of evaluations and/or narrative descriptions; resumes; official records; student self-evaluations or reflections; responses from parents,

1. Determine the purpose of the assessment.
2. Identify relevant behaviors and environments.
3. Verify Steps 1 and 2 based on input from student and others important others.
4. Choose appropriate assessment procedures.
5. Modify procedures as needed.
6. Conduct the assessment.
7. Use assessment findings to identify transition goals and objectives.
8. Develop curricular plans to achieve goals.

Figure 1.3. Transition Assessment Model. (From Sax, C.L., & Thoma, C.A. [2002]. *Transition assessment: Wise practices for quality lives* [p. 55]. Baltimore, MD : Paul H. Brookes Publishing Co.; reprinted by permission.)

employers, or other evaluators; and/or audio recordings or photographic records (Thoma & Held, 2002). Portfolios are meant to be portable and can contain electronic or hard copies of the student's work.

Demonstrations of mastery are "typically formal, public performances of student competence and skill that provide an opportunity for a summative or final assessment" (Thoma & Held, 2002). Music, art, and vocational education departments typically use this kind of performance-based assessment when students complete a recital, exhibit of their work, or capstone activity at the end of the year. This technique can also be used for shorter-term, formative assessments to provide information about whether a student is mastering the steps of a complex activity such as learning to solve problems or work through an experiment.

Discourse assessment provides an opportunity for students to verbally describe what they know rather than write about it. In this type of assessment activity, teachers can not only hear students talk about what they learned but can also gather information about their students' abilities to solve problems, think critically, self-evaluate, and engage in metacognitive tasks (i.e., to think about how they think and learn). An oral exam completed at the end of a class is an example of a discourse assessment, but so is the more informal time that a teacher spends with students to "check in" on their progress.

Projects are used frequently in academic classes and serve as opportunities for students to work alone or in groups to tackle question-based assignments. Such activities are often interdisciplinary in nature and provide a chance for students to investigate a question by using a variety of resources and to present their findings in a variety of ways. Projects can be summarized in a written report, a collage or work of art, a multimedia presentation, or a combination of methods.

Profiles "are collections of ratings, descriptions, and summary judgments by teachers and others to give a broad view of student achievement" (Thoma & Held, 2002). A summary of performance is a specific example of a profile that can be used by the student to advocate for support and services after high school.

Evaluating informal and performance-based assessments is an important step in identifying a student's ability to perform given tasks and/or assignments. When using informal or alternative/performance-based assessments, Mr. David found that it was important to organize the evaluation of student achievement through the use of a rubric. Rubrics provide a description of expected performance, which educators can use to provide direct and immediate feedback. Not only do students learn from the feedback they receive from the use of the rubric in grading performance, but the rubric is also a useful tool in guiding a student's understanding of the required components necessary to demonstrate their mastery. Mr. David found a resource that outlined three steps to follow in developing a grading rubric. (An example of a grading rubric can be found in Table 2.2 of Chapter 2.) Those steps include the following (Spinelli, 2012, p. 379):

1. List the critical components or objectives of the learning activity.

2. Determine the criteria to be used for the evaluation scale.

3. Write a description of expected performance.

TRANSITION AS A BACKWARD DESIGN PROCESS

Mr. David found a number of references citing the need to start at the end when it comes to transition assessment. He thought of the quotation attributed to Lewis Carroll (n.d.): "If you don't know where you're going, any road will get you there." So identifying the end—the student's vision for his or her adult life—must be the first step in the transition assessment process. Many assessment strategies can help articulate that broad-based vision, from formal assessments such as the Transition Planning Inventory–Second Edition (Patton & Clark, in press) to informal, curriculum-based assessments such as Whose Future Is It Anyway?–Second Edition (Wehmeyer, Lawrence, Kelchner, Palmer, Garner, & Soukup, 2004) or the *Choicemaker Curriculum* (Martin et al., 2007), to alternative/performance-based assessments such as projects or portfolios that describe a student's vision for adult life. In addition to these assessments, planning strategies such as person-centered planning or student-directed IEP processes can provide an opportunity for a student and his or her transition team to articulate a common vision for the student's postschool outcomes.

Once that common vision is identified, the rest of the transition assessment process can identify the team's current information about the student that has an impact on transition planning, as well as the information still needed to identify concrete transition IEP goals, supports, and services. Mr. David found a planning and summary tool he could use to document transition assessment information and results for each student. This tool is found in the Transition Assessment Planning Tool (see Figure 1.4) as a blank document.

CONCLUSION

This chapter provided an overview of the transition assessment process, beginning with an understanding of the legal requirements under IDEA 2004 and a description of the three kinds of assessment procedures that will be described throughout this book. Three purposes for transition assessment data were described, including the determination of a student's vision for the future, his or her strengths and needs, and eligibility for services from various adult service agencies. In addition, the chapter introduced Mr. David and two students, Chris and Michelle, whose experiences navigating the transition assessment process will be shared throughout this book. Both Michelle and Chris will need very different assessments, and using their examples throughout this book will provide an opportunity to learn about different approaches to the types of assessments (formal, informal, performance based/alternative) within each of the different transition domains (employment, postsecondary education, community living, etc.). Unfortunately, this book will not be able to provide examples of every assessment strategy or instrument that exists—nor will it be able to provide examples of how these strategies will work for students who have needs that differ from those of Michelle and Chris—but the combination of concrete examples, tips and strategies, frameworks for organizing your transition assessment efforts, and resource lists of tools and web-based resources should provide a solid foundation for your work.

FOR FURTHER INFORMATION

National Secondary Transition Technical Assistance Center (NSTTAC): http://www .nsttac.org.

This resource provides an annotated bibliography of transition assessment tools and resources.

Transition Assessment Planning Tool

Transition Assessment Checklist						
Transition domains	Academic connection/ information	Transition assessments	Adminis- tered by	Assessment format	Environment	Results
Self- determination						
Employment						
Community						
Transportation						
Recreation and leisure						
Postsecondary education						
Additional domains						

Self-check:

Student strengths and preferences considered
Multiple means of expression, representation, and engagement
Multiple opportunities
Multiple and/or appropriate environment
Multiple evaluators
Academic links

Figure 1.4. Transition Assessment Planning Tool.

Adapted from Thoma, C.A., Bartholomew, C., Tamura, R., Scott, L., & Terpstra, J. (2008, April) *UDT: Applying a universal design approach to link transition and academics.* Boston, MA: Preconference workshop at the Council for Exceptional Children Convention. In *Demystifying Transition Assessment* by Colleen A. Thoma, Ph.D., and Ronald Tamura, Ph.D. (2013, Paul H. Brookes Publishing Co., Inc.)

Iowa Model for Age-Appropriate Transition Assessment: http://transitionassessment .northcentralrrc.org/IowaModel.aspx.

This resource includes questions that help guide choosing appropriate transition assessments.

National High School Center at American Institutes for Research: http://www.better highschools.org.

This resource includes guidelines for using data to determine whether students are prepared for colleges and careers.

2

Academic Assessment

Colleen A. Thoma, Roberta Gentry,
Kimberly Boyd, and Karren Streagle

Students with and without disabilities are subject to a number of formal and informal assessments designed to evaluate their progress in mastering academic content and meeting academic standards for their age and grade level. In fact, general education reforms mandated through the No Child Left Behind Act (NCLB) of 2001 (PL 107-110) as well as the work in many states to adopt a set of Common Core State Standards (CCSS) can leave teachers and transition coordinators like Mr. David with questions about how to address transition assessment, planning, and instruction while simultaneously assuring access to the general education curriculum for all students. This was the first challenge in addressing transition assessment that confronts transition teams: finding a way to creatively combine the two seemingly competing goals for assessment and instruction. There are a number of connections between academic and transition assessment, and that connection should be strengthened as the principles set forth by the CCSS identify knowledge and skills necessary to help students become "college and career-ready" (Kendall, Pollack, Schwols, & Snyder, 2007).

More than 40 states across the country have adopted the CCSS, a set of academic standards released in June 2010 that "outline the knowledge and skills in English language arts and math that students in grades kindergarten through 12 are expected to learn to be prepared for college and careers" (Kober & Rentner, 2012, p. 1). But even when states decide not to adopt the CCSS, they are still required to make changes to their state assessments in order to demonstrate that students exiting their high schools are college and career ready. One way they can do this is by asking local colleges or universities to verify that state academic standards for high schools continue to be challenging enough to ensure that high school graduates are ready for college work. The other option is for them to work with "other states to set standards that research determines prepares students for the rigorous academic challenges of college and to enter the workforce ready to succeed" (U.S. Department of Education, National Center for Education Statistics, 2011, p. 1). *College and career ready* refers to preparing students with "the knowledge and skills needed to enroll and succeed in credit-bearing, first-year courses at a postsecondary institution (such as a two- or four-year college, trade school, or technical school) without the need for remediation" (ACT, 2010, p. 1).

How can educators make sense of the standards? *Unwrapping the standard* refers to a process of reading a standard to identify what students need to achieve the following:

1. Know (the concepts or content)

2. Be able to do (the skills)

3. Identify the context (how educators will teach the concepts and skills; Ainsworth, 2003, p. 5)

Once the specific standard and grade-specific indicators are chosen, the next step is to pinpoint the key concepts and skills. Ainsworth (2003) recommends underlining concepts, circling skills, and highlighting using different colors—or, on electronic versions of the standards, changing the font (e.g., italics for concepts and boldface for skills) can also work. A graphic organizer such as the one in Figure 2.1 can be used to represent the information in a way that makes sense. The information represented in the graphic organizer can then be used to decide on the specific lessons, activities, or units of instruction that will be used to teach the concepts and skills.

Grade level and content area: *Writing applications, grades 8–10*

Standard(s) and Indicators:

A. Produce letters (e.g., business letters, letters to the editor, cover letters for job applications) that follow the conventional style appropriate to the text, include appropriate details, and exclude extraneous details and inconsistencies.

B. Write a persuasive piece that states a clear position, includes relevant information, and offers compelling evidence in the form of facts and details.

Concepts—need to know:

Letters
- Business letters
- Letters to the editor
- Cover letters for job applications
- Conventional style
- Details: appropriate; extraneous; inconsistencies

Persuasive pieces
- Clear position
- Relevant information
- Compelling evidence: facts; details

Skills—be able to do:

- Produce (letters; job applications)
- Follow (conventional style)
- Include (appropriate details; relevant information)
- Exclude (extraneous details; inconsistencies)
- Write (persuasive piece)
- State (clear position)
- Offer (compelling evidence; facts and details)

Topics or context—activities to teach the concepts and skills:

- Write letters to an editor and/or a congressional representative on a topic of interest related to national policy and its impact on local or state level.
- Develop a resume and write a letter of application for a specific job; complete online job applications.

Figure 2.1.   Graphic organizer for "unwrapping" content standards. (*Source:* Ainsworth, 2003.)

FORMAL ACADEMIC ASSESSMENTS

Transition to school (college) or work can be difficult for students. The tasks of choosing a job and preparing for work, deciding to go to college or trade school, and deciding where to live and with whom are all areas of the decision-making process and present youth with disabilities the challenge of having to make complex decisions. In order to assist students with these decisions, information gleaned from formal, informal, and performance-based academic assessments is used to guide this process. The data gathered from these assessments assist in matching students' abilities and preferences to appropriate academic, vocational, and functional educational programs, and the assessment data provides useful information about a student's abilities and strengths. Good planning should address academic achievement and functional performance in order to facilitate the movement from school to postschool activities (Virginia Department of Education, 2010).

The performance of students on CCSS testing is one example of an important formal assessment process designed to measure student academic achievement and preparation. Academic assessments assist educators and transition specialists in determining the instructional needs of a student that will move the student toward his or her postsecondary goals. Data gathered from academic assessments also provides information for the present level of academic and functional performance and provides necessary guidance to write measurable postsecondary goals.

Formal academic achievement tests measure aptitude, achievement, intelligence, and adaptive skills. Since Chris's postschool plans are to attend college, updated educational and intelligence measures will be completed to assist his college counselor with planning and accommodations in the college setting. Mr. David knew that college counselors usually wanted testing that was less than one year old, so he requested updated testing in those areas. This assessment, typically conducted by a school psychologist or a medical doctor (depending on the nature of a student's disability) serves to 1) document that the student (in this case, Chris) has a disability that would qualify him for academic accommodations at his chosen university and 2) identify appropriate adaptations and accommodations that would address his specific learning needs. See Chapter 5 for more specifics about that process.

Academic assessments for Chris and other students who might be interested in transitioning to postsecondary education also need to include formal admission testing such as the Scholastic Aptitude Test (SAT) and/or the ACT. The SAT was designed to measure aptitude, or the potential to do well, in a college setting. In comparison, the ACT was designed to measure achievement in the academic areas of English, mathematics, reading, science, and writing. Efforts have been made to align the ACT test with the CCSS, and benchmarks were identified to determine whether a specific student's scores meet the criteria for being college and career ready. Mr. David found that Chris's scores in the areas of English, mathematics, and science met and/or exceeded those benchmarks while his reading and writing scores did not. A comparison of the benchmarks and Chris's scores on the ACT are included in Table 2.1.

In addition to the tests that are usually administered during the eligibility and college admission processes, Mr. David found the following assessments to be helpful:

- *Armed Services Vocational Aptitude Battery* (ASVAB; United States Military Entrance Processing Command, 2005) is a norm-referenced assessment given by the military to measure academic ability and predict occupational success. Eight test areas (general science, arithmetic reasoning, word knowledge, paragraph comprehension, mathematics knowledge, electronics information, auto and shop information, and mechanical

Table 2.1. Benchmarks and scores

Academic area	ACT college readiness benchmarks*	Student scores
English	18	18
Mathematics	22	27
Science	24	25
Reading	21	20
Writing	7	5

*ACT College Readiness Benchmarks for English, Mathematics, Science, and Reading are copyrighted by ACT, Inc. (2010) and reproduced by permission.

comprehension) are combined into three composites or career exploration scores. These scores help students understand their verbal, math, science, and technical skills in comparison to those of other students in the same grade. This test is available online for free at http://www.military.com/ASVAB.

- *Career Ability Placement Survey* (CAPS; Knapp & Knapp, 1976) is an individualized, norm-referenced measure of abilities related to various vocational fields. It measures eight vocationally relevant abilities (mechanical reasoning, spatial relations, verbal reasoning, numerical ability, language usage, word knowledge, perceptual speed and accuracy, and manual speed and dexterity) within the context of the entry requirements for a variety of jobs and careers.

- *Reading-Free Vocational Interest Inventory* (RFVII-2; Becker, 2000) is a norm-referenced measure of vocational interests presented in a reading-free format designed for use with individuals from ages 12 through 62 and may be administered in a group situation. Examinees view a series of picture triads of individuals involved in a variety of work-related activities and select the picture of the activity that most interests them. This assessment would be especially beneficial for Michelle, since there is no reading involved.

Formal Academic Assessments for Students with Significant Intellectual Disabilities

Alternate assessments based on alternate academic achievement standards (AA-AAS) are designed to measure the academic achievement of students with significant intellectual disabilities as a mechanism for including these students in school accountability systems. These alternative standards are based on general education academic content standards in reading, math, and science. However, the academic content standards for students with significant intellectual disabilities have been reduced in complexity (U.S. Department of

Postsecondary Considerations

Be sure that you consider postsecondary options for all students with disabilities, including those who would not have been able to have this opportunity in the past. Encouraging all students with disabilities to take formal academic assessments such as the ACT and/or SAT keeps the doors open for all. In addition, it has been shown that there is a link between having an individualized education program (IEP) goal of going to postsecondary education and employment later according to data collected through the National Longitudinal Transition Study–2 (NLTS-2) survey (NLTS-2, 2008).

In some states, students who take AA-AAS are not eligible to earn a regular high school diploma (U.S. Department of Education, 2005). Check with your school testing coordinator or director of special education to determine whether their participation would affect their graduation and diploma status. In addition, as more states adopt the CCSS and their inclusion of multiple assessment procedures, it will be important to keep up-to-date in regard to the impact on graduation requirements for students with more significant support needs. Check the web site for the common core standards (http://www.corestandards.org), and refer to the department of education in your state to keep up-to-date on the latest developments.

Education, 2005). These alternate academic content standards are intended to address the content areas of reading, math, and science, but they do not necessitate the depth or breadth of knowledge required of students in the general curriculum. While AA-AAS differ from state to state, they all fit into one of three main categories: rating scales, performance assessments, and portfolio assessments (Elliott & Roach, 2007). AA-AAS include checklists, observations in structured and unstructured settings, performance assessments, samples of student work, and portfolios (Roeber, 2002).

While students with significant intellectual disabilities are required to take AA-AAS, there is little evidence to suggest a relationship between how students score on these assessments and their postsecondary outcomes (Kleinert, Garrett, Towles, Nowak-Drabik, Waddell, & Kearns, 2002). Researchers have also found that students' IEP goals do not often align with the academic content assessed on AA-AAS (Karvonen & Huynh, 2007). Therefore, it is important for special education teachers working with students with significant intellectual disabilities to make connections between the academic content assessed on AA-AAS, what is included in a student's transition IEP, and the functional skills necessary for success after high school.

INFORMAL ACADEMIC ASSESSMENTS

In addition to using formal assessments, informal assessments provide useful and meaningful information about a student's academic achievement. Formal tests cannot measure important elements of transition planning such as identifying whether an individual can read social cues in various work, recreation, or social settings, and they do not address whether an individual can modify behavior to meet the demands of multiple environments (Black & Ornellas, 2001). For this level of understanding, informal assessments are needed. Informal assessments are nonstandardized measures that can be modified and adjusted in order to gain useful information about a student. Informal assessments include reports of observations made by teachers, parents, employers, and other school personnel as well as grade- or school-wide assessments, interest inventories, file reviews,

Did You Know?

Reading comprehension is an academic skill often assessed on AA-AAS. Reading comprehension skills relevant to a student's transition IEP may include reading and understanding a restaurant menu or job application. These functional life skills can be important to a student with a significant intellectual disability when he or she leaves high school. This type of linkage between a student's transition IEP and the academic content assessed on AA-AAS can make AA-AAS scores more meaningful to the transition process.

Did You Know?

In a survey of state education agencies, 50% of those responding indicated that they require specific assessments to be used as part of a student's age-appropriate transition assessment. Those assessments include the following: the Enderle Severson Transition Rating Scale, social skills rating forms, the Life Centered Education (LCE) Transition Curriculum competency-based assessments, self-determination assessments, the SAT, the Next Step Curriculum student portfolio, learning style assessments, and job analyses.

situational assessments, rating scales, and curriculum based-measurement. Teachers can use informal assessments to gather information across a variety of instructional settings that helps them determine a student's basic academic skills, how the student learns best, and the student's personal preferences and work habits (Sitlington, 2008).

Informal assessments are especially helpful when developing transition plans, since they generally provide information that is easier to link to specific transition and academic goals. They also can provide information that is more likely to address the needs of students with more significant support needs, like Michelle, since they often provide opportunities for students to represent their knowledge and skills in multiple ways.

Since Chris didn't meet the benchmarks for the reading and writing components of the ACT test, it was important for Mr. David to consider what other assessments might provide information to guide Chris's transition planning process. He considered a range of formal assessment options but targeted a learning style assessment for its ability to provide insight into how Chris learns best—information that would enable future academic instruction to build upon his strengths. A learning style assessment would provide information Chris could later use to advocate for accommodations and modifications he might need while in college. Mr. David found an online learning style assessment that both Chris and Michelle could access at http://www.learning-styles-online.com/inventory. They each then used the link to learn more about their preferred learning style and about strategies that could help them develop individualized learning goals and identify possible adaptations that would work for them. Figure 2.2 is the screen-shot from Chris's learning style inventory.

Some examples of other informal assessments include the following:

- *C.I.T.E. Learning Style Inventory* can be found at http://www.harding.edu/arc/PDF/CITE.pdf. Another inventory called the Visual, Aural, Read/Write, Kinesthetic (VARK) inventory can be found at http://www.vark-learn.com/english/page.asp?p=questionnaire

- *The Brigance Transition Skills Inventory* (TSI; Brigance, 2010) is a criterion-referenced instrument designed to evaluate skills in areas generally taught within life-skills programs, including those involved in speaking and listening, money and finance, functional writing, food, words on signs and warning labels, clothing, health, telephone, travel and transportation, and reading. It was designed for students in eighth grade through adulthood. This instrument scores these areas as mastered or not mastered.

- *Choosing Outcomes and Accommodations for Children* (COACH) is a guide to educational planning for students with disabilities (Giangreco, Cloninger, & Iverson, 2011), and provides a variety of informal assessment strategies that can help teachers plan instructional supports and delivery methods that meet their academic needs.

For User: Chris

This page displays the results of your learning styles inventory. You can also select options below to compare your styles with anybody who has shared their results with you.

Your results

The scores are out of 20 for each style. A score of 20 indicates the style is used often.

Style Scores

Style	Score
Visual	13
Social	16
Physical	11
Aural	14
Verbal	12
Solitary	12
Logical	10

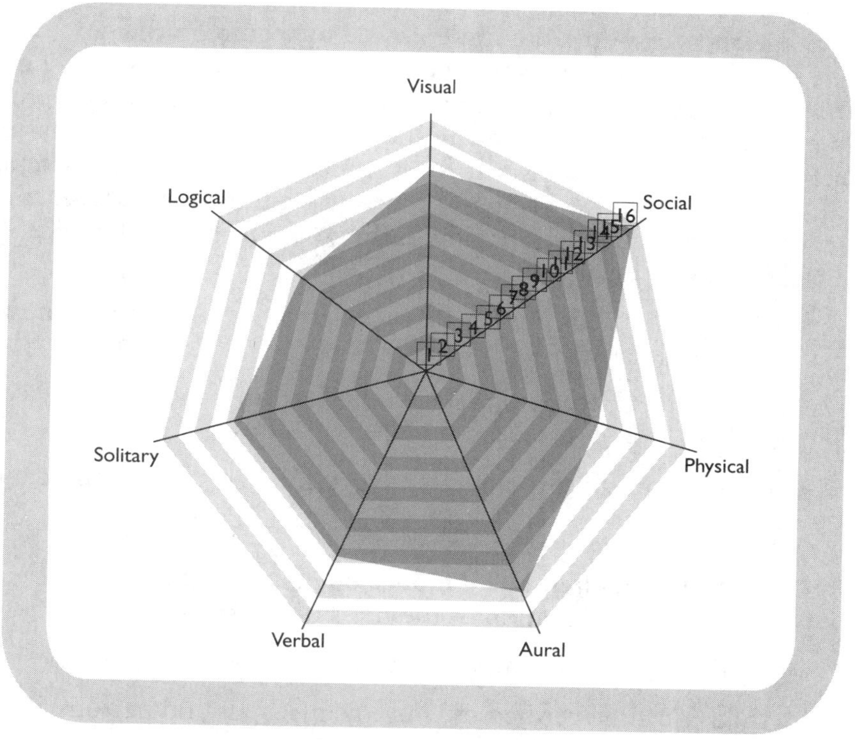

Figure 2.2. Learning Styles Inventory—Results Page. (From Advanogy.com. [2012]. *Results from learning styles inventory.* Retrieved from http://learning-styles-online.com; reprinted by permission.)

- *Ansell-Casey Life Skills Assessment* (ACLSA; Casey, 1994–2005) is an individually administered self-reporting assessment of life skill mastery across nine domains (daily living, self-care, work and study skills, social relationships, housing and money management, communication, home life, work life, and career planning). This assessment is available free online and can be completed by the student, parents, or teachers. A free report is provided as well as lesson plans. This assessment is available at http://www.caseylifeskills.org/pages/assess/assess_index.htm.

- *Study skills inventory* (Hoover & Patton, 2007) provides information that helps teachers rate students on study skills such as listening, test taking, note taking and outlining, time management, and organization. Teachers rate students on a scale from "not proficient" to "highly proficient." The book also helps teachers develop instructional strategies that address a range of study skills.

When deciding what information to gather, Mr. David understands that the right questions need to be asked so as to be certain that the information collected addresses identified domains or skill areas necessary for student-focused planning. Mr. David will use both formal and informal assessments to determine his student's needs and to construct meaningful and appropriate plans for the student. Then this data can be used to answer questions such as the following: What are the student's strengths related to the student's postsecondary vision? How are the student's functional and academic skills? Are the student's school programs and classes aligned with their postsecondary vision? What knowledge and skills does the student currently demonstrate in each of these areas? What knowledge and skills does the student need to acquire in the next few years?

The academic achievement data provided through formal and informal assessments is the starting point for the present level of performance, which provides the IEP team with a clear understanding of where the student is performing relative to where he or she wants to go. In determining which assessments (or combination of assessments) to use, Mr. David referred to the position statement on transition assessment of the Division on Career Development and Transition (Sitlington, Neubert, & Leconte, 1997), which identified eight guiding statements:

1. Assessment methods must be customized to specific types of information needed for upcoming decisions.

2. Methods must be appropriate to the learning and response characteristics of the individual.

3. Assessment must incorporate assistive technology or accommodations when necessary.

4. Assessments must occur in natural environments.

5. Assessment measures must produce outcomes that influence the development, planning, and implementation of the transition process.

6. Methods must include multiple, ongoing activities that sample behavior and skills.

7. Methods must be verified by multiple methods and persons.

8. Assessment results must be stored in user-friendly formats.

ALTERNATIVE OR PERFORMANCE-BASED ACADEMIC ASSESSMENTS

Many of the formal academic assessments discussed earlier in the chapter are formatted as multiple-choice tests, in which a question or statement is followed by four or five answer choices. Alternative academic assessments are intended to provide opportunities for students to demonstrate what they know in ways that serve as an "alternative" to paper-and-pencil tests. They are also sometimes referred to as performance assessments. These specialized assessments can be as individual as the students who benefit from them. Herein lies the strength of these assessments. Mr. David realized he could work with his students to develop academic assessments that would allow them to demonstrate what they knew in the way that best suited their strengths. He was only limited by his imagination and the imagination of his students. His students enjoyed helping create these assessments and felt empowered that they were able to demonstrate their knowledge in a way that was meaningful and successful to them. However, freedom and creativity tie into the challenges of alternative assessments as well. Alternative assessments take a lot of time to develop, and they can be time consuming to score.

Alternative assessments are most successful when the teacher is well acquainted with a student's strengths and challenges in communication and how he or she understands concepts. It also helps to know a student's other areas of strength, such as art, music, computers, and so on. Allowing a student to demonstrate what he or she knows through art, music, computers, or other means can be a powerful way for the student to demonstrate his or her academic knowledge. It is also important to collaborate with the student who is taking an alternative assessment to ensure that he or she understands the skills and concepts to be demonstrated and the expectations of the teacher.

As already mentioned, alternative assessments can be as individual as the students who take them. Students may use performing, visual, or graphic arts to demonstrate their knowledge. They may create posters, models, or slide presentations. Alternative assessments may also be as simple as a conversation with a teacher about the content to be assessed. For example, in English class, Michelle developed a slide presentation to illustrate her understanding of the themes of Shakespeare's play, *Romeo and Juliet*, and she dressed in costume to represent one of the characters from the play while she shared her presentation with the class. She was able to program her communication device to "speak" parts of the slide presentation for emphasis. Chris was allowed to apply his love of music to illustrate his understanding of the themes of *Romeo and Juliet*. He wrote a song and performed it for the class. Although alternate assessment can be time consuming, students feel a great sense of accomplishment when they are able to show their knowledge in a way that is unique and successful for them.

Wiggins and McTighe (2011, pp. 10–11) provided guidance for assessment that clearly demonstrates the strength of alternative, performance-based assessments, recommending that in the best learning design, assessments are the following:

- *Clear.* There is no mystery as to the performance goals or standards.
- *Diagnostic.* They check for prior knowledge, skill level, and misconceptions.
- *Authentic.* Students demonstrate their understanding through real-world applications.
- *Purposeful.* Assessment methods are matched to achievement targets.
- *Ongoing.* Assessments occur over time with descriptive feedback.
- *Useful as learning opportunities.* Students are expected to engage in trial and error, reflection, and revision.
- *Student-directed.* Students have the opportunity to self-assess.

APPLYING THE PRINCIPLES OF UNIVERSAL DESIGN FOR LEARNING TO ACADEMIC ASSESSMENT

Within a typical classroom, a teacher uses many strategies from the principles of universal design for learning (UDL). The UDL approach is based on research designed to understand how the brain learns and how some people learn differently (Bowe, 2000). This research

TIP

Consider developing a portfolio assessment to help students collect academic work samples, both formal and informal, to showcase their strengths. Students including both those with mild disabilities and those with more significant disabilities can use portfolios to demonstrate their academic abilities. For those students who will graduate from high school, it is helpful to include a sequence of required high school courses. Each semester, the student is able to have a visual picture of his or her progress toward graduation. Students with more significant disabilities can also keep a portfolio of their academic work and a plan of required benchmarks that will lead to independent living and employment. The most powerful part of a portfolio is teaching the student to reflect on his or her academic work—a skill needed for postsecondary education and training. For more information, go to Portfolios for Student Growth, Gallaudet University, National Center for Deaf Education's web site: http://www.gallaudet.edu/clerc_center/ information_and_resources/info_to_go/transition_to_adulthood/portfolios_for_student_growth.html.

demonstrates the success of using a mixture of technologies to enable students with diverse learning needs to succeed academically (Orkwis & McLane, 1998). Instruction and assessments designed using a UDL approach have three primary characteristics (CAST, 2007):

- Multiple means of representation, which give students various ways to acquire information and knowledge (materials and instructional delivery)

- Multiple means of expression, which provide students with alternatives to demonstrate what they know (assessment)

- Multiple means of engagement, which focus on students' interests to offer appropriate challenges and increased motivation and engagement

When thinking about the various activities that Mr. David could recommend teachers implement in their classrooms, he thought of group work, independent work, student projects, hands-on activities, test reviews, homework reviews, and many more. All of these activities can be considered academic assessments, can be presented with the use of UDL, and can be used as data to help support the transition process. When UDL is used for academic assessment, it "reduces or removes barriers (to help provide) an accurate measurement of learner knowledge, skills, and engagement" (CAST, 2011). Mr. David used the three main principals of UDL to guide teachers in transforming their classrooms into fully functional UDL environments.

Principle 1: Provide Multiple Means of Representation

Teachers could provide various formats of academic assessments and allow students to choose which one best met their needs. Mr. David was also sure to remind teachers to provide assessments in the student's primary language, and he found that electronic versions of assessments could be translated into different languages more easily than translating a test into each language separately. Mr. David had learned that helping students in accessing prior knowledge would help in the comprehension, generalization, and long-term retention of the new information, and he therefore made it a habit to encourage teachers to use this strategy whenever possible.

When Mr. David helped a teacher adapt a test or quiz, the result often looked different from the original. He used different colored paper, different fonts, and different font sizes, provided both a pen-and-paper version and an audio recorded version, incorporated graphs/pictures/diagrams to support the question being asked (or the multiple-choice answer being provided), and made use of tactile opportunities whenever applicable. Mr.

David found this to be a better way to assess students on what they learned. It provided an opportunity for students to illustrate what they learned in the way that they felt most comfortable with. He also believed it helped alleviate student test anxiety and, in turn, raised their test scores.

Homework assignments looked very different when Mr. David adapted these assignments for teachers. Mr. David encouraged teachers to allow students to e-mail their answers, discuss or work with a partner, record answers, write answers in the traditional format, and use any other methods that they felt comfortable with. Again, he found that providing multiple ways for students to respond to assessments led to an increase in participation, an increase in scores, and a general increase in the happiness of the classroom environment. In addition, this translated into more accurate information to use for developing transition goals.

Principle II: Provide Multiple Means of Action and Expression

Mr. David recommended to teachers that when they assigned group work and presentations, they should allow students to choose how they present the information. Students could be given time to discuss how they would like to present—first with their group members and then with the teacher. The teacher could provide guidance regarding which methods of presentation made more sense given the information that they were presenting.

Mr. David was also a big advocate for the use of technology within the classroom. He understood that we are living in a technology savvy world and that most students needed or preferred to use some piece of technology to help complete their work. In addition, improving one's skills in the use of technology was a skill that translated to greater independence in a number of goals for adult postschool outcomes. He encouraged teachers to use a range of technology including computers, iPads, switches, computer overlays for touch screen access, different types of software, calculators, spellcheckers, approved social networking, discussion boards, and so on.

When teaching or presenting information to his students, Mr. David encouraged teachers to use visuals and hands-on manipulative materials daily. He encouraged them to make sure the tools they used were available for student use when they were completing assignments or doing any kind of assessment that would reflect what they had learned.

Principle III: Provide Multiple Means of Engagement

Mr. David encouraged teachers to create activities and assessments that varied in regards to how challenging they were and then allow students to choose among a variety of levels. This allowed teachers to assess all of the students on their own comfort levels while still assessing them all on the same topics/ideas that were taught.

When providing feedback in the form of observations or number/letter grades, Mr. David recommended that teachers provide more immediate and descriptive feedback to students, rather than focus on assigning a final grade, so that students could improve their performance. He encouraged teachers to focus on formative assessment rather than summative (or final) assessment by providing students the following information regarding their performance:

- An exemplar or standard for comparison

- A description of how the student's performance compares to the exemplar

- Sufficient information that the student can use to improve performance (Wiggins & McTighe, 2006)

Using grading rubrics along with providing an example (or exemplar) of the desired performance is one way that Mr. David recommended that teachers follow these criteria for effective feedback. Table 2.2 is an example of a grading rubric for evaluating student performance for a presentation. This rubric, along with a videotaped presentation that students could access on their laptop, provided a mechanism for providing feedback as well as an exemplar.

Universal Design for Transition

As you can see, Mr. David has put a lot of thought, time, and effort into helping teachers use a UDL approach in their classrooms. He also learned how to expand a UDL approach to transition assessment, planning, and instruction. This has been called universal design for transition (UDT) (Thoma, Bartholomew, & Scott, 2009). UDT "expands the concepts of barrier-free methods and design to include their application to the design, delivery, and assessment of educational services related to the transition from school to post-school for students with disabilities" (Thoma et al., 2009, p. 9). The UDT framework includes the characteristics of UDL described above but adds additional characteristics that reflect best practices for transition planning and services, including the following:

- Multiple transition/life domains

- Multiple means of assessment

- Student self-determination

- Multiple resources/perspectives (Thoma et al., 2009)

Using a UDT framework requires that educators change their instructional planning to address two questions that high school students often voice in class: "Why do I need to learn this?" and "When will I ever need to use this information?" Research supports

Table 2.2 Sample presentation rubric

	1	2	3	4
Subject Knowledge	Lacks a grasp of the information: unable to answer questions about the subject	Is uncomfortable with information and can answer only rudimentary questions	Is at ease with expected answers to all questions but fails to elaborate	Demonstrates full knowledge (more than required) by answering all class questions with explanations and elaborations
Elocution	Mumbles, mispronounces terms, speaking volume too low to be heard in back of classroom	Voice is low; incorrectly pronounces terms; audience has difficulty hearing presentation	Voice is clear; pronounces most words correctly; most audience members can hear	Uses a clear voice and correct, precise pronunciation of terms so that audience can hear presentation
Organization	Audience cannot understand presentation because there is no sequence of information	Jumps around in topic; audience has difficulty following presentation	Presents information in logical sequence that audience can follow	Presents information in logical, interesting sequence that audience can follow
Eye Contact	Reads all of report with no eye contact	Occasionally uses eye contact but still reads most of report	Maintains eye contact most of the time but often returns to notes	Maintains eye contact with audience, seldom returns to notes
Mechanics	Presentation has five or more spelling errors and/or grammatical errors	Presentation has three or four misspellings and/or grammatical errors	Presentation has no more than two misspellings and/or grammatical errors	Presentation has no misspellings or grammatical errors

the use of this approach as a way to increase student academic achievement, engagement in learning, and understanding of the connection between the lesson and the students' transition goals (Scott, Saddler, Thoma, Bartholomew, Alder, & Tamura, 2011). Armed with this information, Mr. David can work with teachers to identify the functional applications of the material they were trying to teach and, in particular, help students make the connection to their goals for adult life.

INVOLVING PARENTS IN ACADEMIC ASSESSMENT

When families are involved as partners in their children's education and transition plans, outcomes are seen in regards to the students, the families, the schools, and the communities in which they live (Kochhar-Bryant & Bassett, 2002). One of the many ways parents and students can be involved in the education and transition process is through assessment.

When discussing how to use standards-based assessments as a team, there are some specific strategies that parents and students can use to become more active in their respective roles. One of the first things Mr. David asks his parents/families to focus on is how they can help analyze and use the results to create future academic and transition goals (Kochhar-Bryant & Bassett, 2002). He guides them in how to focus specifically on mastery of content and how to recognize whether an assessment assesses content that is needed for the student to accomplish his or her goals. Mr. David also helps the parents to understand how well their child performed in regards to the standard that was being assessed. He then asks the parent to discuss how the assessment aligns with their child's specific goals and needs and if they have any additional information that could be provided to support the results of the assessment. The additional information may be verbal, a recollection of previous assessments that Mr. David may be unaware of, or an observation that the parents saw within their home.

Before Mr. David can gain information from the parents/family, he believes he must make them comfortable and involved as members of the IEP team. They cannot be outsiders who simply attend the meeting, and their opinions and input cannot fall on deaf ears. Mr. David encourages his parents/families to speak about the accommodations that are appropriate for their students to use on assessments. He also offers to help the parents/families work with their children's teachers to get a closer look at the types of assessments that they are preparing their children for. This then allows the parents/families to work on practicing for the assessment outside of the school environment.

Parents can be helpful in summarizing their child's functional ability outside of the classroom, particularly as it relates to study skills, time management, planning skills, and problem-solving skills. A list of specific skills and information parents can provide that can inform the transition planning process include the following:

- Career interests
- Test preparation/study skills
- Budgeting/money management skills
- Recreation and leisure interests
- Friendships and relationships with others
- Transportation use and preferences
- Community activities and/or volunteer opportunities
- Time management skills
- Technology use at home

The Parent Survey of Student's Academic-related Skills form (see Figure 2.3) provides a parent survey form that Mr. David developed for teachers to send home and have parents complete. He could then use this information in combination with student academic assessment information to help with identifying transition IEP goals that would support student goals for their future.

Involving the parents/families in assessments and knowledge about how the information gained from them can help their child can provide a much more complete picture of student abilities, preferences, and interests. Mr. David found that it is an important step in gathering all of the information needed on a student in order to help make that student's transition plan and personal transition goals work for that student.

Outcomes for students with disabilities are most successful when IEP planning involves the family and considers the family's cultural values and beliefs (Artiles, Trent, & Palmer, 2004; Kim & Morningstar, 2005). Williams (2008) suggested the following steps to work with families of students with cultural and linguistic diversity:

1. Identify the cultural values that are embedded in your interpretation of the student's difficulty or in the recommendation of service. For example, why do you expect Johnny to live independently from his family?

2. Find out if the family recognizes and values those same beliefs and values or how they may differ.

3. Acknowledge and respect all cultures, and explain the basis for your professional belief.

4. Through discussion and collaboration, determine the most effective way to adapt your professional interpretations and recommendations to the value system of the family.

COLLABORATING WITH OTHERS IN ACADEMIC ASSESSMENT

Transition coordinators need to collaborate with general education teachers responsible for teaching academic content as well as with students and parents to be sure they are considering all relevant information to develop a comprehensive transition plan. General educators not only know the standards well; they also can provide information about how a student performs in academic settings—information that would be helpful for planning a transition to postsecondary education settings and adult life. Figure 2.4 is an example of a study skills inventory that provides the kind of information that Mr. David found to be helpful for transition planning, focusing on student performance in class as well as test-taking strategies (Spinelli, 2012, pp. 421–24). Mr. David asked Chris's teachers to complete this survey regarding his performance in academic classes.

Summarizing Academic Information

Mr. David knew that the best way to assure that this range of academic information was used to guide transition planning was to summarize the information collected by the various assessment partners: general education teachers, special educators, psychologists, parents, and the students themselves. In his research, he learned about the requirements for completing a summary of performance, which is used at the end of a student's high school career to help support the student in advocating for supports and services he or she may need from a variety of adult service providers. He learned that the "goal of the Summary of Performance is to enhance postschool outcomes for students with disabilities by providing them with relevant information about their academic achievement and

Parent Survey of Student's Academic-related Skills

Parents, please complete this form based on the level of independence your son/daughter exhibits in the following skills related to academics. Please answer each question based on how much independence your son or daughter typically demonstrates in performing the various tasks, using the following key:

1. *Completely independent* (typically doesn't need reminders or support to complete task)

2. *Somewhat independent* (might need reminders or general prompting to complete task)

3. *Is able to complete task with support*

4. *Is able to complete some of the task with support*

5. *Does not attempt to complete task*

6. *Is not expected to complete task*

7. *Would not be able to complete task*

Skill	1	2	3	4	5	6	7
Area: test preparation							
-Set up/choose an area conducive to study?							
-Gather and organize study materials prior to beginning to study?							
-Develop a study plan that addresses the type of test and the material to be covered?							
-Looks up unfamiliar vocabulary to understand meanings?							
-Space studying over an extended period of time rather than cram for tests?							
-Use memory strategies to help with learning/remember key material?							
-Can identify accommodations needed for tests in specific content areas?							
Area: Career Awareness							
-Can identify one or more jobs that he/she would like to do?							
-Can identify preferences and interests for work environments (that is, out-door/indoor jobs, working alone vs. as part of a team, etc.)							
-Can identify preferences based on prior work or other experiences							

Figure 2.3. Parent survey of student's academic-related skills.

(continued)

Parent Survey of Student's Academic-related Skills (continued)

-Has had a job in the past YES or NO, and please provide more information about the job and how long your son or daughter held that job							
-Can access transportation to get to and from work							
-Can read a bus schedule							
-Can get up on time (or otherwise plan day) to get to work on time							
Area: money management/budgeting							
-Has received a paycheck or allowance in the past							
-Uses money to make purchases							
-Plans for purchases by saving							
-Compares costs for an item that he/she wants to purchase							
-Is aware of the cost of various living expenses							
Area: affective/interpersonal skills							
-Is able to compromise with others							
-Is able to cooperate with others							
-Is curious about the world							
-Is dependable							
-Is enthusiastic to learn new things							
-Is persistent with a task							
-Is tolerant of change							
-Is able to work with others to complete a task							
-Is able to use the computer to complete tasks							
-Is able to use the internet to research a specific topic							
-Is able to complete reports using a computer							
-Uses a schedule or calendar to remember deadlines							
-Uses technology to communicate with others (e-mail, text messages, social media, etc.)							
-Has a friend or friends and makes plans to spend time with them							

Comments: Please use this section to provide any explanation to any of the above items:

Thank you for your assistance with this. The information will help us develop a comprehensive transition plan for your son or daughter. Please return this completed form to your son/daughter's teacher by the following date: _____.

Demystifying Transition Assessment by Colleen A. Thoma, Ph.D., and Ronald Tamura, Ph.D.
Copyright © 2013 by Paul H. Brookes Publishing Co. Inc. All rights reserved.

Study Skills Inventory

Student Name: _____ Grade: _____

Completed by: _____ Date: _____

Directions: Rate each item using the scale provided. Base the rating on the individual's present level of performance.

Study Skill	Rating			
	Not Proficient (NP)	Partially Proficient (PP)	Proficient (P)	Highly Proficient (HP)
Reading Rate				
Skims	0	1	2	3
Scans	0	1	2	3
Reads at rapid rate	0	1	2	3
Reads at normal rate	0	1	2	3
Reads at study or careful rate	0	1	2	3
Understands the importance of reading	0	1	2	3
Listening				
Attends to listening activities	0	1	2	3
Applies meaning to verbal messages	0	1	2	3
Filters out auditory distractions	0	1	2	3
Comprehends verbal messages	0	1	2	3
Understands importance of listening skills	0	1	2	3
Graphic Aids				
Attends to relevant elements in visual material	0	1	2	3
Uses visuals appropriately in presentations	0	1	2	3
Develops own graphic material	0	1	2	3
Is not confused or distracted by visual material in presentations	0	1	2	3
Understands the importance of visual material	0	1	2	3
Library Usage				
Uses cataloging system (card or computerized) effectively	0	1	2	3
Can locate library materials	0	1	2	3
Understands organizational layout of library	0	1	2	3
Understands and uses services of media specialist	0	1	2	3
Understands overall functions and purposes of a library	0	1	2	3

Figure 2.4. Study Skills Inventory.

Study Skills Inventory. Note. From *Teaching Study Skills to Students with Learning Problems: A Teacher's Guide for Meeting Diverse Needs, 2nd Ed.* (pp. 50–54), by J. J. Hoover & J. R. Patton, 2007, Austin, TX: PRO-ED. Copyright 2007 by PRO-ED, Inc. Adapted with permission. In *Demystifying Transition Assessment* by Colleen A. Thoma, Ph.D., and Ronald Tamura, Ph.D. (2013, Paul H. Brookes Publishing Co., Inc.)

(continued)

Study Skills Inventory *(continued)*

Study Skill	NP	PP	P	HP
Understands importance of library usage skills	0	1	2	3
Reference Materials				
Can identify components of different reference materials	0	1	2	3
Uses guide words appropriately	0	1	2	3
Consults reference materials when necessary	0	1	2	3
Uses materials appropriately to complete assignments	0	1	2	3
Can identify different types of reference materials and sources	0	1	2	3
Understands importance of reference materials	0	1	2	3
Test Taking				
Studies for tests in an organized way	0	1	2	3
Spends appropriate amount of time studying different topics covered on a test	0	1	2	3
Avoids cramming for tests	0	1	2	3
Organizes narrative responses appropriately	0	1	2	3
Reads and understands directions before answering questions	0	1	2	3
Proofreads responses and checks for errors	0	1	2	3
Identifies and uses the clue words in questions	0	1	2	3
Properly records answers	0	1	2	3
Save difficult items until last	0	1	2	3
Eliminates obvious wrong answers	0	1	2	3
Systematically reviews completed test to determine test-taking or test-studying errors	0	1	2	3
Corrects previous test-taking errors	0	1	2	3
Understands importance of test-taking skills	0	1	2	3
Note Taking and Outlining				
Uses headings (and subheadings) appropriately	0	1	2	3
Takes brief and clear notes	0	1	2	3
Records essential information	0	1	2	3
Applies skill during writing activities	0	1	2	3
Uses skill during lectures	0	1	2	3
Develops organized outlines	0	1	2	3
Follows consistent note-taking format	0	1	2	3
Understands the importance of note-taking	0	1	2	3
Understands the importance of outlining	0	1	2	3
Report Writing				
Organizes thoughts in writing	0	1	2	3
Completes written reports from outline	0	1	2	3
Includes only necessary information	0	1	2	3
Uses proper sentence structure	0	1	2	3
Uses proper punctuation	0	1	2	3
Uses proper grammar and spelling	0	1	2	3

(continued)

Study Skills Inventory. Note. From *Teaching Study Skills to Students with Learning Problems: A Teacher's Guide for Meeting Diverse Needs, 2nd Ed.* (pp. 50–54), by J. J. Hoover & J. R. Patton, 2007, Austin, TX: PRO-ED. Copyright 2007 by PRO-ED, Inc. Adapted with permission. In *Demystifying Transition Assessment* by Colleen A. Thoma, Ph.D., and Ronald Tamura, Ph.D. (2013, Paul H. Brookes Publishing Co., Inc.)

Study Skills Inventory *(continued)*

Study Skill	NP	PP	P	HP
Proofreads written assignments	0	I	2	3
Provides clear introductory statement	0	I	2	3
Includes clear concluding statements	0	I	2	3
Understands importance of writing reports	0	I	2	3
Oral Presentations				
Freely participates in oral presentations	0	I	2	3
Organizes presentations well	0	I	2	3
Uses gestures appropriately	0	I	2	3
Speaks clearly	0	I	2	3
Uses proper language when reporting orally	0	I	2	3
Understands importance of reporting orally	0	I	2	3
Time Management				
Completes tasks on time	0	I	2	3
Plans and organizes daily activities and responsibilities effectively	0	I	2	3
Plans and organizes weekly and monthly schedules	0	I	2	3
Reorganizes priorities when necessary	0	I	2	3
Meets scheduled deadlines	0	I	2	3
Accurately perceives the amount of time required to complete tasks	0	I	2	3
Adjusts time allotment to complete tasks	0	I	2	3
Accepts responsibility for managing own time	0	I	2	3
Understands importance of effective time management	0	I	2	3
Self-Management				
Monitors own behaviors	0	I	2	3
Changes own behavior as necessary	0	I	2	3
Thinks before acting	0	I	2	3
Is responsible for own behavior	0	I	2	3
Identifies behaviors that interfere with own learning	0	I	2	3
Understands importance of self-management	0	I	2	3
Organization				
Uses locker efficiently	0	I	2	3
Transports books and other materials to and, from school effectively	0	I	2	3
Has books, supplies, equipment, and other materials needed for class	0	I	2	3
Manages multiple tasks or assignments	0	I	2	3
Uses two or more study skills simultaneously when needed	0	I	2	3
Meets individual organizational expectations concerning own learning	0	I	2	3
Understands importance of organization	0	I	2	3

Summary of Study Skills Performance: _____

Study Skills Inventory. Note. From *Teaching Study Skills to Students with Learning Problems: A Teacher's Guide for Meeting Diverse Needs, 2nd Ed.* (pp. 50–54), by J. J. Hoover & J. R. Patton, 2007, Austin, TX: PRO-ED. Copyright 2007 by PRO-ED, Inc. Adapted with permission. In *Demystifying Transition Assessment* by Colleen A. Thoma, Ph.D., and Ronald Tamura, Ph.D. (2013, Paul H. Brookes Publishing Co., Inc.) *(continued)*

Study Skills Inventory *(continued)*

Directions: Summarize in the following chart the number of not proficient (NP), partially proficient (PP), proficient (P), and highly proficient (HP) subskills for each study skill. The number next to the study skill represents the total number of subskills listed for each area.

Study Skill	NP	PP	P	HP
Reading rate (6)				
Listening (5)				
Graphic aids (5)				
Library usage (6)				
Reference materials (6)				
Test taking (13)				
Note taking and outlining (9)				
Report writing (10)				
Oral presentations (6)				
Time management (9)				
Self-management (6)				
Organization (6)				

Summary comments about student study skills: _____

Rubric for Evaluating Impact of Study Skills Usage

Study Skill	1 Minimal Usage of Skill/No Impact on Learning	2 Some Usage/ Irregular Impact on Learning	3 Consistent Usage/ Regular Impact on Most Learning	4 Daily Usage/No-ticeable Impact on Most Daily Learning
Reading rate	1	2	3	4
Listening	1	2	3	4
Graphic aids	1	2	3	4
Library usage	1	2	3	4
Reference materials	1	2	3	4
Test taking	1	2	3	4
Note taking and outlining	1	2	3	4
Report writing	1	2	3	4
Oral presentations	1	2	3	4
Time management	1	2	3	4
Self-management	1	2	3	4
Organization	1	2	3	4

Comments: _____

Study Skills Inventory. Note. From *Teaching Study Skills to Students with Learning Problems: A Teacher's Guide for Meeting Diverse Needs, 2nd Ed.* (pp. 50–54), by J. J. Hoover & J. R. Patton, 2007, Austin, TX: PRO-ED. Copyright 2007 by PRO-ED, Inc. Adapted with permission. In *Demystifying Transition Assessment* by Colleen A. Thoma, Ph.D., and Ronald Tamura, Ph.D. (2013, Paul H. Brookes Publishing Co., Inc.)

Academic Summary Form

Student name		Date of birth	
Address		Phone (home)	
		Phone (cell)	
Parent/guardian			
Anticipated graduation date		Diploma type	
Disability category		Date of last eligibility	

Grade	GPA	Class rank	Credits
9		/	
10		/	
11		/	
12		/	

SAT scores	Date	Verbal	Non-verbal	Writing	Composite

ACT scores	Date	English	Math	Science	Reading	Writing

Woodcock-Johnson	Date of test	Grade	Age
Test	Grade equivalent	Age equivalent	Age standard scores
Broad reading			
Broad math			
Broad written lang.			
Broad gen. know			

Employment/career goals	
Post secondary education goals	
Independent living goals	
Leisure and recreation goals	
Results of personal interest inventory	
Academic strengths	
Academic challenges	
Accommodations for success in class	
Accommodations for success on tests	
Results from learning style survey	

Figure 2.5.   Academic summary form.

From Davidsen, D.B., & Streagle, K.D. (2011). Developing the transition curriculum. In Wehman, P. (Ed.), *Essentials of transition planning* (p. 46). Baltimore, MD: Paul H. Brookes Publishing Co.; adapted by permission. In *Demystifying Transition Assessment* by Colleen A. Thoma, Ph.D., and Ronald Tamura, Ph.D. (2013 by Paul H. Brookes Publishing Co., Inc.)

functional performance" (Kochhar-Bryant, 2007, p. 77). The Summary of Performance (SOP) is often completed during a student's final year of high school, so while it assists with the transition to postschool options for students, it does not provide assistance with transition assessment. Rather, it is a summary of the assessment information collected along the way. Mr. David found a link to a model on the web site of the Council for Exceptional Children at http://www.cec.sped.org/pp/pdfs/SOP.pdf.

However, Mr. David wanted a way to summarize academic information collected each year that would allow him to share it with the transition IEP team as they identified transition goals for the coming year. The Academic Summary Form (see Figure 2.5) is an academic summary form that worked for him, successfully allowing him to summarize information about individual students.

CONCLUSION

Transition assessment does not typically include a focus on academic assessment, but these types of assessments are completed for students with and without disabilities on an ongoing basis. Their results do help inform transition planning, and this chapter provided guidance for educators to make the most of this data and identify ways to solidify the link between academic and transition assessment through the use of a universal design for learning and transition approach.

3

Self-Determination Assessment

Colleen A. Thoma

The connection between student self-determination and improved transition outcomes is well-documented in the literature. In fact, student self-determination has been linked to such diverse transition outcomes as employment (Martorell, Gutierrez-Rechacha, Pereda, & Ayuso-Mateos, 2008; Wehmeyer & Schwartz, 1997), community living (Wehmeyer & Palmer, 2003), postsecondary education (Thoma & Getzel, 2005), and more globally to an improved quality of life (Nota, Ferrari, Soresi, & Wehmeyer, 2007; Shogren, Lopez, Wehmeyer, Little, & Pressgrove, 2006). Student self-determination, or involving students in identifying the vision and goals for their adult lives (Wehman & Brooke, 2012; Wehmeyer, Field, & Thoma, 2012; Wehmeyer & Shogren, 2013), appears to be at the heart of effective transition assessment, planning, and educational services and supports. This chapter will provide guidance for educators on how to conduct an assessment of students' self-determination as well as how to use that information to 1) improve their level of self-determination and 2) inform the transition assessment, planning, and service delivery processes.

SELF-DETERMINATION

Before really focusing on how to assess a student's level of self-determination, it is important to understand what is meant by self-determination and why it is so critical for effective transition planning and instruction. The definition of self-determination has evolved over the years, with the most recent and widely accepted definition coming from Wehmeyer (2006): "Self-determined behavior refers to volitional actions that enable one to act as the primary causal agent in one's life and to maintain or improve one's quality of life" (p. 177).

In addition to this definition of self-determination, Wehmeyer and Field (2007, p. 3) describe four essential characteristics of self-determined behavior:

- The person acts autonomously.

- The behavior or behaviors are self-regulated.

- The person initiates and responds in a psychologically empowered manner.

- The person acts in a self-realized manner.

Although these characteristics describe self-determined behavior, it is important to note that most individuals (with and without disabilities) work on acquiring and/or refining

Did You Know?

What does it mean to "act as the primary causal agent in one's life"? There can be some discrepancy in interpretation of this part of the definition of self-determination. It does not mean doing everything yourself; nor does it mean doing whatever one wants without regards to consequences. It does mean making choices and decisions and setting goals for oneself that honor an individual's preferences and interests while taking into account the realities and consequences of one's actions. For example, when choosing to take a vacation, one can drive a car, which includes a large variety of choices, decisions, and autonomy, or one can decide to fly to a destination, which involves conforming to many more rules and regulations. One gives up independent control to travel farther or faster (flying) than would be possible using a method that provided more independent control (driving). Self-determination is the ability to make the ultimate decision of how one gets to the destination rather than the degree of autonomy one has in making that journey. This analogy can be helpful in determining a distinction between self-determination (causal agency) versus autonomy (doing it all yourself). The reality is that most of us don't choose to do everything on our own; we instead envision an adult life in which a number of collaborative and/or interdependent relationships exist.

these skills throughout their lives and that, ideally, the development of self-determination begins in early childhood. The "level" of self-determination that one displays is influenced by his or her "age, opportunity, capacity, and circumstances" (Wehmeyer & Field, 2007, p. 4).

Consider the two students, Michelle and Chris, whose transition assessment processes are described throughout this book. Both of them can and should be expected to demonstrate self-determination in their transition planning process, although they have very different functional self-determination levels and will need different supports to communicate and achieve their goals for adult life. No two people will have the same ability to demonstrate self-determined behavior, and this helped Mr. David begin to identify ways that he could support both Michelle and Chris in their transition from high school to adult life. Although they both have very different strengths and needs related to self-determination, it was important for their transition planning team to identify their current strengths and facilitate the development of self-determination skills for them both.

Self-determination is a global term that refers to a number of core component skills, and assessment of self-determination (and, ultimately, helping to facilitate the development of a student's self-determination) typically focuses on these separate component skills. For a student like Michelle, who had a number of needs related to self-determination, it can be helpful to break the concept down into these separate components and then prioritize which ones to address first. These component skills and their definitions are included in Table 3.1.

Lastly, it is important to note that students from culturally and linguistically diverse backgrounds may have some additional needs related to self-determination. Researchers currently agree that self-determination in transition planning is important for all students, but many of them also hypothesize that there may be some very different ways in which the core component skills are used by students from culturally and linguistically diverse (CLD) backgrounds. Shogren (2011) conducted a review of the literature on self-determination and found that few studies investigated whether there were differences in the operational definitions of self-determination, the ways in which self-determination should be taught, and/or the impacts of self-determination on postschool options for students from diverse backgrounds. Shogren (2011) provides a list of implications for

Table 3.1.   Self-determination core component skills

Skill	Definition
Choice making	Identifying a preference between two known options
Decision making	Identifying a preference between three or more options
Problem solving	Identifying a preference or course of action when the options are unknown or unclear
Goal setting and attainment	Determining a goal for the future, the steps to attain the goal, and a timeline for doing so
Self-regulation/self-management	Understanding a desired behavior and working to monitor one's ability to demonstrate that behavior in a given situation or situations
Self-advocacy and leadership skills	Having the ability to speak up for oneself and one's rights as well as influencing the actions of others
Positive perceptions of control, efficacy, and outcome expectancies	Believing that one's actions influence an outcome, that one has the ability to learn the necessary skills or perform the necessary actions, and that using those skills will result in positive outcomes
Self-awareness	Demonstrating the ability to understand one's strengths and weaknesses and to understand one's response to the people and activities in one's environment
Self-knowledge	Possessing the ability to use knowledge of self to improve one's quality of life

From Thoma, C.A., Bartholomew, C.C., & Scott, L.A. (2009). *Universal design for transition: A roadmap for planning and instruction.* (p. 33). Baltimore, MD: Paul H. Brookes Publishing Co.; adapted by permission.

educators to use in facilitating self-determination of students from CLD backgrounds, which are outlined in the teacher tip below.

FORMAL SELF-DETERMINATION ASSESSMENTS

There are a number of formal self-determination assessment instruments developed to determine an individual student's level of self-determination, including the Arc's Self-Determination Scale (Wehmeyer & Kelchner, 1995), the AIR Self-Determination Scale (Wolman, Campeau, DuBois, Mithaug, & Stolarski, 1994), and the Self-Determination Assessment Battery (Hoffman, Field, & Sawilowsky, 2004). Each of these assessments was developed a formal assessment, meaning that they are standardized so that they are administered in a specific way, have formal scoring procedures, and were normed with a large number of individuals to ensure assessment validity and reliability. A summary of these self-determination assessments, as well as access to some of them, can be found through the Zarrow Center at the University of Oklahoma.

The ARC self-determination scale (Wehmeyer & Kelchner, 1995) was developed to assess the level of self-determination of students with intellectual or cognitive disability, such as Michelle. Questions in each of the four sections are presented in different formats; students can complete the assessment independently or have questions read to them. The four sections include autonomy, self-regulation, psychological empowerment, and self-realization. Once the student completes the assessment, educators follow directions to

---

TIP

When supporting the self-determination of students from diverse cultural and linguistic backgrounds, it is critically important to find ways to involve their families as partners. Families help students shape their cultural identities, which can also impact how they operationalize self-determined behavior. The self-determined learning model of instruction (Wehmeyer, Agran, Hughes, Martin, Mithaug, & Palmer, 2007) is a strategy that can be used in school as well as at home or in the community to support student self-determination.

Zarrow Center for Learning Enrichment

The Zarrow Center for Learning Enrichment at the University of Oklahoma (http://www.ou.edu/content/education/centers-and-partnerships/zarrow.html) seeks to "facilitate successful secondary and postsecondary educational, vocational, and personal outcomes for students and adults with disabilities" (Zarrow Center, n.d.). Under the link for "Self-determination assessment," the Zarrow Center makes available free copies of self-determination assessment scales as well as information about interpreting a student's self-determination scores. The free assessments available online include the AIR Self-determination Scales, including a Spanish language version for students (http://www.ou.edu/content/education/centers-and-partnerships/zarrow/self-determination-assessment-tools/air-self-determination-assessment.html), the ARC Self-determination Scale (http://www.ou.edu/content/education/centers-and-partnerships/zarrow/self-determination-assessment-tools/arc-self-determination-scale.html), and the Field & Hoffman Self-determination Assessment Battery (http://www.ou.edu/content/education/centers-and-partnerships/zarrow/self-determination-assessment-tools/field-and-hoffman-self-determination-assessment.html). Dr. James Martin is the current Zarrow Chair and directs the activities and research of the Zarrow Center.

---

convert the scores to percentile ranks to determine a student's self-determination profile. The scoring manual (also available online) provides direction for determining how to use the student profile information to develop instruction or otherwise facilitate self-determined behavior.

Michelle's performance on the ARC Self-determination Scale indicated that she scored higher in self-realization and psychological empowerment than in either autonomy or self-regulation. Mr. David felt that Michelle's score in the self-regulation area may have been lower than it should have been because of her struggle with communication—that is, she might not be able to communicate to others that she was able to identify the correct response to different parts of the scenario. Because of this, Mr. David planned to find a way to observe Michelle in situations similar to the scenarios from the test in order to supplement the information obtained from this assessment, determining whether she actually did have the ability to act in a self-regulated manner to. Michelle's score in the area of autonomy was very revealing: Mr. David found that Michelle felt that others may be too quick to jump in to help her when she wanted an opportunity to try to do some of these activities herself. This was information that would be useful in developing Michelle's annual transition plan.

The AIR Self-determination Scale (Wolman et al., 1994) consists of three similar assessment tools completed by the student, parent, and teacher, respectively. Each of these components is designed to determine a student's self-determination knowledge and skills. Having the scale completed by all three people provides a comprehensive evaluation of student self-determination by providing information about a student's opportunity to use and improve those skills at school and home. This can be particularly useful when students have multiple experiences and/or are held to different expectations in different settings. Chris's parents had provided more opportunities for him to make his own decisions and act autonomously than his life at school had typically given him, so their assessment of his self-determination was higher than his teacher's evaluation. This difference opened a dialogue that helped all three gain a better understanding of Chris's abilities: His teachers started giving him more opportunities to act autonomously, and his parents found ways to introduce more structure to his after-school study time. Each of these steps brought the supports closer in line with the skills that Chris needed to be self-determined.

A third example of a self-determination assessment is the Self-determination Assessment Battery (Hoffman et al., 2004). This assessment also provides opportunities for students, educators, and parents to participate in completing components of the assessment. Wehmeyer, Field, and Thoma list five instruments that make up the self-determination assessment battery:

1. Self-Determination Knowledge Scale Pretest, forms A & B
2. Self-Determination Parent Perception Scale
3. Self-Determination Teacher Perception Scale
4. Self-Determination Observation Checklist
5. Self-Determination Student Scale (2012; p. 177)

Once each component of the assessment is completed, Mr. David would need to compile this information to score each assessment and identify student needs for skill development as well as opportunities to use existing knowledge and skills. This assessment provides more detail about a student's self-determination skills, but the time needed to complete the full assessment made it difficult to use on large numbers of students with disabilities. Instead, it might be used with students for whom more detailed information is needed, such as those who have more difficulty in providing reliable answers to questions about what they do, so that the observation of their behavior in various settings was necessary to obtain a clear picture of their self-determination skills.

CURRICULUM-BASED SELF-DETERMINATION ASSESSMENTS

A variety of curriculum materials were developed in the 1990s to teach one or more of the core component skills of self-determination and can be particularly useful in the acquisition phase of learning. Many of those curricula are still published today, in updated versions, including *Next S.T.E.P.* (Halpern, Herr, Wolf, Doren, Johnson, & Lawson, 2000), *Choicemaker* (Martin, Huber-Marshall, Maxson, Jerman, Hughes, Miller, & McGill, 2000) and *Steps to Self-Determination* (Field & Hoffman, 2005). Not only do these curricula include lesson plans and strategies helpful for teachers and students to use; they also include assessments designed to identify existing self-determination skills as well as those skills that were missing from an individual student's repertoire. But rather than just have a self-determination score, the assessments developed as part of these curricula help educators link the assessment score to educational goals and lesson plans they can use in classroom settings to improve students' use of and/or increase in self-determination skills. Not only are these available through the publishers; the Zarrow Center also provides a comprehensive description of some of these curricula on their web site under "Self-determination education materials" at http://www.ou.edu/content/education/centers-and-partnerships/zarrow/self-determination-education-materials/choicemaker-self-determination-materials.html.

Assessment of current skills and abilities is a critical first step in the teaching process. The assessment process should provide information about what a student can do as well as information about the context of the setting in which the skill is assessed. Educators should remember that a specific component skill such as self-advocacy might be demonstrated in one situation and not in others, making it imperative that the assessment process includes multiple settings and multiple perspectives. Discrepancies between settings and/

or evaluator perspectives provides valuable information that can guide further assessment to determine the aspects of the setting, the situation, and/or the individuals with whom the student interacts that support or act as barriers to self-determination. This information can then be used to identify the strategies that promote the development and use of self-determination for that individual.

There is one interactive curriculum for self-determination titled *Whose Future Is It?* (Wehmeyer & Palmer, 2011) that was originally a paper-and-pencil format (that version is available free of charge on the Zarrow Center's web site at http://www.ou.edu/content/education/centers-and-partnerships/zarrow/self-determination-education-materials/whos-future-is-it-anyway.html) and is now available as a software package published through the Attainment Company. This curriculum includes a student reader, workbook, and instructor's guide along with the software. Such a software program would be a great resource for students like Michelle, who struggle with reading. This program provides an opportunity for her to hear the text and use a switch to access and complete the various learning activities. The curriculum helped her complete assessments of her preferences and interests, identify goals for the future, and draft annual goals and objectives to help her meet those long-term goals. Completing the components of the curriculum provided Mr. David with an opportunity to assess Michelle's use of self-determination core component skills as well as her growth after receiving instruction designed to increase self-determination skills.

PERFORMANCE-BASED SELF-DETERMINATION ASSESSMENTS

Other assessment procedures can help assess student self-determination, typically focusing on specific component skills rather than the more global self-determined behavior. In schools, students like Chris and Michelle demonstrate aspects of self-determined behavior by engaging in one or more of the following: participating in transition individualized education program (IEP) meetings through a student-directed IEP or person-centered planning process, using problem-solving strategies such as the self-determined learning model of instruction (Wehmeyer, et. al., 2007) to set goals and measure progress, or participating in assessments designed to identify preferences and interests. This section of the chapter will introduce educators to each of these strategies.

Student-Directed IEP

Thoma, Saddler, Purvis, and Scott (2010) define a student-directed IEP process as a "range of methods, strategies, and approaches that are designed to provide support to a student with disabilities in participating in the IEP process to the maximum extent possible" (pp. 8–9). Student direction of the IEP process is a great way to learn and practice core component skills of self-determination. In fact, Mr. David learned that a student-directed IEP approach can increase student self-determination in general (Test, Mason, Hughes, Konrad, Neale, & Wood, 2004) and increase student and parent participation in the meeting itself (Martin, Van Dycke, Greene, Gardner, Christensen, & Woods, 2006). Mr. David once again found that the web site of the Zarrow Center at the University of Oklahoma contained a variety of resources that he could access at no cost to organize his efforts to implement student-directed IEP processes for Chris and Michelle. Each of them had different strengths related to their ability to lead their IEP meeting, but Mr. David found resources that he could use to help facilitate their direction of the process. He also found the Checklist for Student-Directed IEP Meeting (see Figure 3.1) that could be used by Chris (independently) and

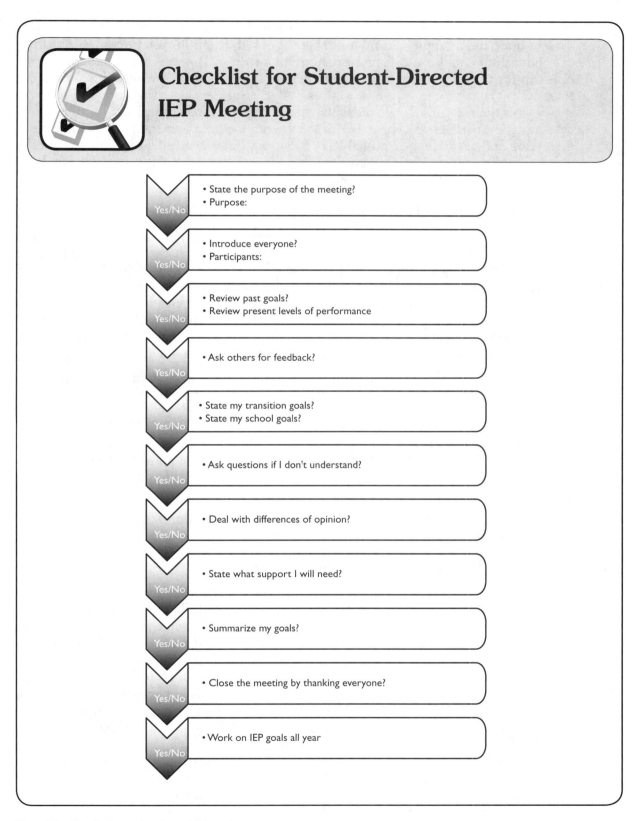

Checklist for Student-Directed IEP Meeting

Yes/No
- State the purpose of the meeting?
- Purpose:

Yes/No
- Introduce everyone?
- Participants:

Yes/No
- Review past goals?
- Review present levels of performance

Yes/No
- Ask others for feedback?

Yes/No
- State my transition goals?
- State my school goals?

Yes/No
- Ask questions if I don't understand?

Yes/No
- Deal with differences of opinion?

Yes/No
- State what support I will need?

Yes/No
- Summarize my goals?

Yes/No
- Close the meeting by thanking everyone?

Yes/No
- Work on IEP goals all year

Figure 3.1. Checklist for student-directed IEP meeting.

From Martin, J.E., Marshall, L.H., Maxson, L.M., & Jerman, P.L. (1996). *The self-directed IEP*. Longmont, CO: Sopris West; adapted by permission. In *Demystifying Transition Assessment* by Colleen A. Thoma, Ph.D., and Ronald Tamura, Ph.D. (2013, Paul H. Brookes Publishing Co., Inc.)

by Michelle (with support) as a means to evaluate his or her own ability to implement a student-directed IEP approach and his or her use of self-determination through the process.

Educators could use a listing of the steps of the IEP process as a self-monitoring checklist for students and transition team members to use during the meeting itself to cue them as to the next step of the process as well as to self-evaluate their progress through the steps of the meeting. While the first assessment provides an evaluation of student self-determination through the entire IEP process (from meeting preparations through implementation and evaluation of annual IEP goals), this quick assessment focuses specifically on the meeting itself. The Checklist to Determine What Worked in an Individualized Education Program (IEP) form (see Figure 3.2) is an example of this.

Self-Determined Learning Model of Instruction

The self-determined learning model of instruction (SDLMI; Mithaug et al., 1998) is a strategy that can be used to teach a problem-solving approach that students can use in a variety of different settings to take control of their learning. The SDLMI is truly an authentic assessment procedure, as it requires that students perform a task that adults do almost daily: solve problems. It certainly won't take long for educators to reflect back and remember the last time they needed to solve a problem or were asked to help a friend or colleague solve one of their own. Being an adult can mean that one will be faced with multiple problems to solve, and the SDLMI can help with that. The SDLMI has three phases:

1. *Set a goal.* Identify what you want to accomplish, what your strengths and needs are in relation to accomplishing the goal, and what you can do to address the needs.

2. *Take action.* Identify the specifics of a plan to solve the problem or accomplish the goal.

3. *Adjust goal or plan.* After implementing the plan, this phase focuses on evaluating your progress in meeting the goal and, for goals that were not met, identifying what changes need to be made to the original goal as the three-phase cycle begins again.

Figure 3.3 is an example of a student worksheet used by Chris to set a goal for improving his grades in his English class (where writing book reports was particularly difficult for him to complete on time).

One-Page Example for Summarizing Information

Participating in a student-directed IEP process can be a great way for students to improve their self-determination skills, but for some students, it can be a scary process. It is important to identify resources that help students feel more comfortable and organized so that they share information they want to use to guide their goals and to plan for the future. Mr. David also wanted to find a way to help students increase their self-awareness and self-knowledge skills, which are such an important component of self-determination. He looked for ways that, through the use of an authentic assessment activity, he could assess how well Michelle and Chris knew themselves. He knew that most job interviews included questions or prompts such as the following: "Tell me about yourself"; "What are the skills that you bring to this job?"; and even "What would you say you would like to change about yourself?". Mr. David worked with the school's guidance counselors to develop a list of sample interview questions and used a discourse assessment strategy to assess the students' skills while also working with them to build on their strengths. Chris was able to do this without extra supports, but Michelle needed a way to communicate this information

Checklist to Determine What Worked in an Individualized Education Program (IEP)

How did my IEP go?

Date of IEP: _____

I worked hard to get ready for the IEP meeting by learning to speak up for myself and be a good team leader/member. After the meeting is over, I will look at the following checklist to help me decide what I need to improve for next time (remember, there is always room for improvement), and what I need to do in the post-meeting follow-up.

Yes	No	Item to consider
❏	❏	Were all the people I invited to the meeting there?
❏	❏	Was I introduced to everyone I didn't know?
❏	❏	Did I make sure everyone else at the meeting was introduced?
❏	❏	Did I have a chance to do all of the meeting that I practiced/prepared?
❏	❏	Did other team members listen to me?
❏	❏	Did I get to talk about the things I like to do? About things I don't like to do?
❏	❏	Did I get to talk about my goals for the future?
❏	❏	Did I talk about the things I do well? About things I don't do well?
❏	❏	Did we find ways to help me address my learning needs/challenges/struggles?
❏	❏	Did I talk about academic accommodations and adaptations?
❏	❏	Did I address my access to the general education curriculum?
❏	❏	Did I address my transition goals (if I'm at least 16 years old)?
❏	❏	Did I have a say in who was invited to the meeting?
❏	❏	If not, are there people I would like to invite to the next meeting?
❏	❏	Does my plan have goals for all the things I think are important?
❏	❏	Is this the best IEP plan for me at this time? (To determine the answer to this question, answer the following questions first.)

Figure 3.2. Checklist to determine what worked as well as what would be improved in an individualized education program (IEP).

(continued)

From Thoma, C.A., & Wehman, P. (2010). *Getting the most out of IEPs: An educator's guide to the student-directed approach* (p. 253). Baltimore, MD: Paul H. Brookes Publishing Co.; reprinted by permission. In *Demystifying Transition Assessment* by Colleen A. Thoma, Ph.D., and Ronald Tamura, Ph.D. (2013 by Paul H. Brookes Publishing Co., Inc.)

Checklist to Determine What Worked *(continued)*

Yes	No	Item to consider
❏	❏	Do I like the classes I am taking?
❏	❏	Am I learning new things in my classes?
❏	❏	Am I learning how to do things in the community?
❏	❏	Am I taking classes with my peers?
❏	❏	Am I learning what I need to become more independent?
❏	❏	Am I learning things that will prepare me for what my life will be like as an adult?
❏	❏	Am I learning how to get along with others?
❏	❏	Am I learning how to work with others?
❏	❏	Am I learning how to speak up for myself?
❏	❏	Am I learning how to solve problems?
❏	❏	Am I learning how to set goals?
❏	❏	Am I learning how to decide if I'm getting where I want to go?
❏	❏	Do I know what I'm good at and can I tell others?
❏	❏	Do I know what kind of help and support I need?
❏	❏	Can I tell others what I need and want?

What supports do I want in my next student-directed IEP meeting?

Support	Keep	Discard	Add
Premeeting (assessment, logistics, organization, practicing, invitations)			
Meeting			
After meeting (share, implement, evaluate, prepare)			

From Thoma, C.A., & Wehman, P. (2010). *Getting the most out of IEPs: An educator's guide to the student-directed approach* (p. 253). Baltimore, MD: Paul H. Brookes Publishing Co.; reprinted by permission. In *Demystifying Transition Assessment* by Colleen A. Thoma, Ph.D., and Ronald Tamura, Ph.D. (2013 by Paul H. Brookes Publishing Co., Inc.)

Name: _Chris_____   Date: _March 1, 2012_____

Phase I: What is my goal?	
Set a goal.	
1. What do I want to learn? *I want to be able to increase my English grade. More specifically, I want to improve my grades on the number of book reports I need to complete this term.*	3. What must change for me to learn what I don't know? *I need to develop a schedule for when the reports are due.* *I need to find ways to make reading more fun.* *I need to stop waiting until the last minute to read and do the reports.* *I need help matching my strengths/preferences and needs with available supports.*
2. What do I know about it now? *I know that I struggle with reading.* *I know that I am easily distracted.* *I know that I usually wait until the last minute.*	4. What can I do to make this happen? *I can work with my teacher to identify steps to complete book reports and create deadlines for completing each step.* *I can spend more time with the librarian, identifying books that would be of greater interest to me and are on my reading level.*

Phase II: What is my plan?	
Take action.	
1. What can I do to learn what I don't know? *I will meet with my teacher to develop a general book report plan with steps and timelines for completion.* *I will meet with the reading specialist in school to identify my reading level.* *I will develop a list of interests that I can use when choosing books for specific assignments.*	3. What can I do to overcome these barriers? *I will meet with the school librarian to identify books that meet the criteria for class, are on my reading level, and better match my interests well in advance of when assignments are due.* *I will list the things that have distracted me from meeting deadlines in the past.* *I will use the general book report plan to identify concrete timelines and steps for each of the book reports as they are assigned.* *I will find resources that the teacher and I can use to develop a book report timeline.* *I will request an evaluation of my reading level well in advance of book report deadlines.*
2. What could keep me from taking action? *I might not be able to follow the timeline that the teacher develops.* *The librarian might not have time to meet with me.* *The reading specialist might not be able to administer additional assessments.*	4. When will I take action? *I will use my study hall time this week to do the initial planning: scheduling meetings, developing a list of reading interests, and researching plans for completing book reports.* *I will get a list of the book report assignments and deadlines from my English teacher by the end of the week.* *I will schedule meetings with the reading specialist, the school librarian, and my teacher within the next 2 weeks.*

(continued)

Figure 3.3. Student worksheet for the self-determined learning model of instruction. (From Thoma, C.A., Bartholomew, C.C., and Scott, L.A. [2009]. *Universal design for transition: A roadmap for planning and instruction* [pp. 37–39]. Baltimore: Paul H. Brookes Publishing Co.; adapted by permission.)

Figure 3.3.   *(continued)*

Phase III: What have I learned?	
Adjust the goal or plan.	
1. What actions have I taken? *I met with the reading specialist, who shared assessment information from previous years. He did not conduct additional assessments.* *I met with the librarian, who provided a list of books on my reading level. I was able to identify books that would fit the requirements for my book report assignments.* *I found a template that I could use to complete the various steps of a book report (including scheduling time to read the book). Then my teacher and I sat down to modify it to meet the criteria for the class.* *I used this template to schedule my work in completing the book reports for the term.*	3. What has changed about what I didn't know? *I know additional resources that can help.* *I was able to complete all book reports with a grade of "B" or better. My English grade improved by using this approach.*
2. What barriers have been removed? *I can talk about my learning style/preferences.*	4. Do I know what I want to know? *I want to learn some of the technologies that were identified by the assistive technology specialist.*

with potential employers. Mr. David found a one-page summary form template originally developed for use in IEP meetings (available at http://www.imdetermined.org/one_pager), which he adapted for her to use for this process. See Figure 3.4 for an example of Michelle's one-page summary form.

Student Indication of Choice/Preference

Some students have a difficult time expressing their choices, preferences, and interests verbally, but educators still need to assess this information and use it to guide the development of transition IEPs. But how can this be done? Educators like Mr. David have found that there are a number of technology options that could help. In addition, Mr. David needed to learn to pay attention to the more subtle ways that students could be communicating this information through their behavior. The following list of strategies recommended by Hughes, Pitkin, and Lorden (1998) and Wehmeyer, Agran, and Hughes (1998) can serve as a good starting point:

- Activation of a microswitch

- Approach toward an object

- Verbalizations, gestures, and effect

- Physical selection of an item

- Task preference

- Time engaged with an item

- Observations of students' responses over time

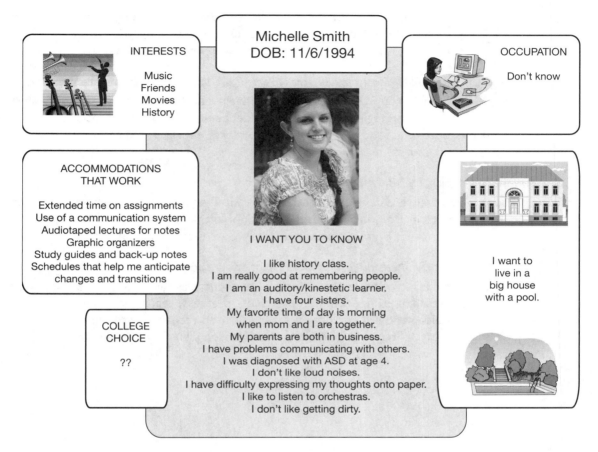

Figure 3.4. Some information about me. (*Source:* Thoma & Wehman, 2010.)

SUMMARY

Mr. David found a number of strategies for assessing student self-determination as well as a number of online resources, such as those available from the Zarrow Center. In fact, many resources of this nature are available—and some of these online resources are included in the information that follows. This component of transition assessment is important and, as was stated earlier, is the heart of transition assessment and planning. Having an understanding of student preferences, interests, strengths, and needs, as well as his or her ability to set and achieve goals and solve problems, is essential in identifying the focus of subsequent transition assessments and ultimately achieving his or her goals for adult life.

FOR FURTHER INFORMATION

I'm Determined Project: http://www.imdetermined.org.

This is a project of the Virginia department of education developed with the intent to increase student self-determination in all grades. It includes training modules for educators, students, and parents as well as a number of downloadable forms, templates, and lesson plans.

Self-Determination Toolkit: http://www.uaa.alaska.edu/centerforhumandevelopment/selfdetermination/index.cfm.

These resources were developed by the University of Alaska–Anchorage's Center for Human Development. Included are guides for students to use in order to increase their self-determination skills, lesson plans for teachers, and other helpful tips.

National Gateway to Self-determination: http://www.aucd.org/NGSD/template/link.cfm.

This is a national group of centers, professionals, and self-advocates who are working to expand the use of strategies that support student self-determination, research on its impact on various outcomes, and steps for scaling up local efforts. It maintains a listing of current strategies and efforts.

Transition Planning Toolkit: http://www.cde.state.co.us/cdesped/TK.asp.

These resources were developed by the Colorado Department of Education to facilitate student self-determination throughout the transition planning and assessment process. Included are checklists, forms, and links to additional resources teachers can use.

Self-determination Synthesis Project: http://sdsp.uncc.edu/home.asp

This site provides information gathered by researchers at the University of North Carolina, Charlotte, regarding evidence-based practices to assess, teach, or otherwise facilitate student self-determination. It provides a listing of these research-based practices, links to the published research literature, and examples of lesson plans that implement these practices.

4

Employment Assessment

Elizabeth Battaglia, Cynthia Nixon, and Ronald Tamura

Preparing students with disabilities for employment is a key component of transition planning. In fact, it has been argued that the purpose of education is to prepare all students for roles that contribute to society—and one of the primary ways most people contribute to society is through their work. While many young adults will graduate from high school and go on to a postsecondary education program, the primary focus for young adults with and without disabilities is to gain employment as a means of support to live as independently as possible. Cameto, Levine, and Wagner (2004) report that preparation for employment is a primary focus of many transition programs for secondary school–aged youth with disabilities.

Research supports the importance of employment-oriented training at the secondary level. Sixty-seven percent of young adults with disabilities who had been out of school 8 years were employed full-time at their most recent job. Ninety-one percent reported holding an average of four jobs during that time, which is comparable to their peers without disabilities. The average wage of those employed full-time was $11.00, and 77% received some type of employment benefit (NLTS-2 Executive Summary, 2011). Employment defines financial independence and success as a productive citizen in the community. Assessing employability skills and career interests is a vital part of transition assessment.

Transition assessment in the employment domain needs to answer a few key questions:

- What job do you want to obtain?

- What are the requirements for that job in terms of education, experience, social skills (or soft skills), and location?

- What are the work conditions for this job in terms of social interaction and setting?

- What kinds of supports will you need in order to meet the requirements of this type of job?

These questions will be addressed in this chapter, along with resources for conducting an assessment of these skills for Michelle and Chris.

IDENTIFYING STRENGTHS, INTERESTS, PREFERENCES, AND EMPLOYMENT OPTIONS

Mr. David knew that Individuals with Disabilities Education Improvement Act (IDEA) of 2004 requires educators to guide students in choosing a career path based on strengths, interests, and preferences. In determining these characteristics, Mr. David, the general education teachers, and/or the transition coordinators need to take into account their students' expressed career interests and observed strengths, interests, and preferences. Mr. David needs to use a variety of formal and informal assessments that were geared toward identifying what types of jobs that Chris and Michelle would like to obtain.

Strengths

Mr. David wanted to answer this question based first on identifying strengths, interests, and preferences for both Chris and Michelle. Since Chris is interested in going to college, the team needed to find out if he has the ability to succeed at the postsecondary level (see Chapter 5). Academically, Chris shows strengths in science and math, so this is the best place to start with his career interest assessment: identifying careers that build on his academic strengths and interests. There are a number of web sites that provide information about career choices, educational requirements, and projected growth in specific geographic areas. The National Association of State Directors of Career Technical Education Consortium (NASDCTEC) has a list of skills needed for the 16 different career clusters (http://www .careertech.org/career-clusters/glance/careerclusters.html). Connecticut Department of Education's School to Career web site has Student Education and Career Record and Evaluation (SECRE) forms that allow for students to see the various skills required for certain career clusters and to record their progress toward mastering the skills (http://www.sde.ct.gov/sde/cwp/view.asp?a=2626&q=320728#frameworks). Another resource is a web site through the U.S. Department of Labor, O*Net Online (http://www.onetonline.org). Students can use this web site to research careers to find the skills and education needed for specific jobs.

There are many web sites that identify career options. Table 4.1 is a list of those sites and how to access them.

Once the results from the assessments were provided, Chris would have the opportunity to participate in job shadowing or community work experiences to gain more information about the identified different career path he has chosen. Mr. David knew that it is critically important to provide real-world experiences as part of any student's employment assessment process. Real work experience provides concrete information of a student's preferences in a way that interest inventories and surveys cannot. If you have never had any of these experiences, it is difficult to answer a question about whether you want to work inside or outside, have a job that requires a great deal of interaction with the public, or find a more solitary position.

Interests

Mr. David decides to first start with The Student Interest Survey for Career Clusters, a quick, 15-minute electronic career interest inventory that will assist Chris in identifying his top three career clusters of interest. Mr. David thought that another formal assessment such as the Kuder–Career Assessment should also be administered, since it provides assessments that are aligned directly with the 16 career clusters found in the electronic survey. The Kuder Skills Assessment will allow Chris to choose the career clusters in which he believes he has the most skills to be successful, and it will then provide him with sample occupations that he can begin exploring. The Kuder Career Search with Person Match will allow Chris to read real-life career stories about individuals with similar interests who have chosen jobs and what their day-to-day job performance requires. Another career inventory that Mr. David found online (see Table 4.1) is called the O*Net Interest Profiler (U.S. Department of Labor, 2002). The O*Net Interest Profiler is an assessment tool that

Table 4.1. Online employment assessments

O*Net assessments

- *Work values assessment:* http://www.onetcenter.org/WIP.html. Download a computerized version or print out a paper copy.
- *Ability profiler:* http://www.onetcenter.org/AP.html. Download the free grading software, assessment, and student answer sheets. This assessment tests a student's aptitude. The software scores and creates a report. Based on the student's performance, the assessment gives a list of jobs for various work zones. O*Net has different work zones that are related to levels of training needed for the job.
- *O*Net profiler:* http://www.mynextmove.org/explore/ip. This is a 60-question computer-based interest inventory that asks the individual to rate specific job activities using a Likert scale from "strongly agree" to "strongly disagree." The score is provided at the end along with links to specific careers aligned with that score.
- *Skills assessment:* http://online.onetcenter.org/skills. This is a simple skills checklist. The survey will provide a list of jobs that fit the student's skills and show whether those particular jobs are in demand. Students can click on the careers to find the job descriptions, abilities needed for each job, and average wages earned in the career.

CareerPath

This is a web site (available at http://www.careerpath.com/career-tests) that offers career interest inventories as well as a planner guide with resources. It requires reading and understanding of specific careers. Students make choices between two career statements. Students can also explore jobs and use the Job Discovery Wizard to enter skills and knowledge levels to match careers.

Clickers

Both clicker programs give the teacher a student's top three Holland codes (theory of career and vocational choices based upon personality types).

- *Career clicker expanded:* (http://www.indianacareerexplorer.com/). It asks questions regarding 300 areas of interest and takes 20 to 25 minutes
- *Career clickers express:* (http://www.in.gov/learnmoreindiana/2734.htm) . It asks questions regarding 50 areas of interest and takes 5 minutes

Drive of Your Life

This is available at http://www.driveofyourlife.org. Signing up is free but will require you to input the town that the student is from. As students answer questions about interests, a virtual car is put together, one piece per answer, providing a visual representation of their progress. When the car is complete, the students will be given a list of jobs based on the assessment. Students then "drive" the car to their top five jobs to find out about a typical day for the job and skills needed.

Career interest: Perfect Career (formerly Career Inventory 2000)

This is available at http://www.theperfectcareer.com. Students need to input an e-mail address to log on. It asks about 160 questions about interests and gives students their Holland codes.

identifies both a career and the amount of training necessary for a wide variety of jobs. The O*Net web site divides all of its jobs into five zones related to the amount of training required for different careers—ranging from zone one, which requires little to no training, to zone five, which requires a doctoral degree. The assessment focuses on nine different areas, including verbal ability, arithmetic reasoning, computation, spatial ability, form perception, clerical perception, motor coordination, finger dexterity, and manual dexterity.

Wehman, Smith, and Schall (2009) state that assessing students with autism can be challenging because of the unique learning characteristics each student exhibits. In testing environments, students with autism can become prompt dependent, focus on irrelevant stimuli, and exhibit limited ability to use learned skills between setting, people, and materials. This can result in an assessment that reports lower skills and abilities than the student actually has. Mr. David must not only account for the issues listed previously but also help Michelle adjust for changes in routines and interactions with coworkers while on a community-based employment placement. Wehman, Smith, and Schall recommend using an assessment planning guide such as the Assessment Planning Guide for Students with Autism form (see Figure 4.1) to assist teachers in gathering all information necessary for the team to discuss and determine the appropriate assessments to administer.

Mr. David knew that Michelle had no idea what type of employment she was interested in and knew how important it was to complete interest inventories that would give Michelle and the team information to make informed choices in the area of careers. Mr. David decided to

Assessment Planning Guide for Students with Autism

Student's name: _____ Date: _____

Team members present:

_____

_____

I. What questions do we have about the student?

1. _____

_____

2. _____

_____

3. _____

_____

II. What type of assessment will help us answer these questions?

❑ Eligibility   ❑ Evaluation of educational practices

❑ Reporting   ❑ Curriculum and program development

III. What learning characteristics will adversely affect these assessment results?

❑ Difficulty with imagining   ❑ Prompt dependence

❑ Difficulty generalizing skills   ❑ Stimulus overselectivity

❑ Difficulty with changes in routines ❑ Communication difficulties

IV. What assessment methods will we use to triangulate the information?

	Assessment method	Team member responsible	Modifications needed
1.			
2.			
3.			

Figure 4.1. Assessment planning guide for students with autism.

From Wehman, P., Smith, M.D., & Schall, C. (2009). *Autism and the transition to adulthood: Success beyond the classroom* (p. 45). Baltimore, MD: Paul H. Brookes Publishing Co.; reprinted by permission. In *Demystifying Transition Assessment* by Colleen A. Thoma, Ph.D., and Ronald Tamura, Ph.D. (2013 by Paul H. Brookes Publishing Co., Inc.)

administer the Reading-Free Vocational Interest Inventory (RFVII-2; Becker, 2000), which is a norm-referenced measure of vocational interests presented in a reading-free format (see Chapter 2). Michelle would view a series of picture triads of individuals involved in a variety of work-related activities and select from each triad the picture of the activity that she would find the most interesting. Mr. David would also administer the Enderle-Severson Transition Rating Scales–Third Edition (ESTRS-3) in order to determine Michelle's preferences and interests in five subscale areas: employment, home living, recreation and leisure, community participation, and postsecondary education. Mr. David also knows that Michelle does not do well on paper-and-pencil types of activities and would like to have a wider variety of interest inventories related to employment. He thought that the Pictorial Inventory of Careers Pathfinder (Borden, 2011) would be a good resource, since this assessment provides a DVD that requires no reading and measures career interests by using live action videos of real-life work scenarios. This inventory focuses on careers in 17 areas and only takes 20–25 minutes to administer. Mr. David will be able to give this inventory to Michelle individually. The PIC Pathfinder will also allow Mr. David to stop and respond to any questions Michelle may have about the careers on the DVD. Once specific career choices have been made, Mr. David will then match Michelle's choices with local businesses to plan for on-site visits and work experience.

Preferences

Mr. David understood that informal assessments are valuable tools in transition assessment. These assessments can include informal inventories (e.g., preference), curriculum-based assessments, direct observations, situational assessments, checklists, questionnaires, and teacher-made assessments. Mr. David also found that there is a wide range of informal transition assessments that are available online (see Table 4.1). Mr. David found that many of these assessments were easy to administer and also quick for the students to take. But Mr. David also realized that both Chris and Michelle needed to experience community-based work experiences and/or job shadowing options to make informed choices on what types of employment they were interested in exploring. Limited time during the school day and poor transportation options often limit educators from making sound decisions on possible employment opportunities. Educators are forced to use work sites at the school or within walking distance, without being able to take into account student preferences. With both Chris and Michelle attending regular classes at their high school, Mr. David had to be creative.

Mr. David chose to create virtual field trips for both Chris and Michelle. By using a digital camera, Mr. David created a series of PowerPoint presentations using several local businesses that were identified as aligning with the results of the interest inventories the students had taken. Each PowerPoint presentation included such information as salary, working conditions, job requirements, benefits, and pictures of the employees performing the required job duties. Mr. David knew that Chris was planning to attend a postsecondary school upon graduation and therefore included part-time jobs that Chris might be interested in while in school. Mr. David would have Chris and Michelle identify the top two employment sites they liked, and the next step would be to arrange visits with the businesses that had been chosen.

Mr. David also remembered that teams should consider administering multiple assessments to a student in order to gather information on various aspects of employment planning, including strengths, interests, and preferences. The Teacher Assessment to Measure Strengths, Interests, and Preferences form (see Figure 4.2) is an informal teacher assessment designed to measure perceived strengths, interests, and preferences and could be administered to both Michelle and Chris.

Teacher Assessment to Measure Strengths, Interests, and Preferences

Name: _____ Date: _____
Grade: _____ Age: _____ Birthdate: _____

1. What is your dream job? _____

2. What is a job in which you would NOT want to do? _____

3. Below put an X next to any career cluster in which you are interested in exploring.

_____ Agriculture, food, and natural resources
_____ Architecture and construction
_____ Arts, audio/video technology, and communications
_____ Business management, and administration
_____ Education and training
_____ Finance
_____ Government and public administration
_____ Health science
_____ Hospitality and tourism
_____ Human services
_____ Information technology
_____ Law, public safety, corrections, and security
_____ Manufacturing
_____ Marketing
_____ Science, technology, engineering, and mathematics
_____ Transportation, distribution, and logistics

4. What type of education are you planning on attending after high school?

_____ 4 year college
_____ 2 year college
_____ Military
_____ Technical school
_____ Certification program
_____ Apprenticeship
_____ On the job training
_____ Other _____

Figure 4.2.   Teacher assessment to measure strengths, interests, and preferences.

(continued)

5. Below put an X next to areas which are your strengths

_____ I'm musical.
_____ I'm artistic.
_____ I'm good at math.
_____ I'm good at creative writing.
_____ I'm able to fix things.
_____ I'm good at science.
_____ I'm good at helping others.
_____ I'm able to organize things.
_____ I'm usually on time.
_____ I'm good at problem solving.
_____ I'm able to do more than one thing at a time.
_____ I am able to adapt to change easily.
_____ I make sure I attend to details.
_____ I'm good with computers.
_____ I can type fast.
_____ I'm persistent (don't give up easily).
_____ I prefer practical things (I like working with my hands).
_____ I like reading books and researching things.
_____ I like to take a leader role.
_____ I'm able to motivate others.
_____ I like learning new things.
other: _____

6. Of the strengths above, list your top two strengths:
   a. _____
   b. _____

7. For each row, pick ONE preference for your work environment and put an X next to it.
   a. _____ Work outdoors   _____ Work indoors
   b. _____ Work alone   _____ Work with others
   c. _____ Fast paced job   _____ Slow paced
   d. _____ Different task each day _____ Complete the same tasks
   e. _____ Work with people   _____ Work with machines
   f. _____ Be a leader   _____ Work in a team
   g. _____ Same hours each day   _____ Different hours each day
   h. _____ Business attire   _____ Casual attire
   i. _____ Work in the daytime   _____ Work at night
   j. _____ Work for a boss   _____ Be a boss yourself
   k. _____ Work in your home   _____ Work outside your home

8. Looking at the list above, what are the top two most important work preferences to you?
   a. _____
   b. _____

Assessing Requirements for a Job

After gathering the information from the assessments administered in the areas of strengths, interests, and preferences, it is important for Mr. David and the appropriate team members (i.e., the job coach and the employment specialist) to take this information and start considering employment options as the next step.

Mr. David knew that education, experience in the job, social skills, and location played a key role in ensuring that both Michelle and Chris were successful after high school. Chris would like to look at a job within the computer software field. Chris excels in school when given a hands-on project to complete that involves working on the computer. At his annual individualized education program (IEP) review last year, Chris stated that he would like to develop video games for a software company. While Chris has his career path chosen, Mr. David knows that Michelle will need a quiet, slow-paced environment that will minimize distractions and stress, both of which often lead to her outbursts. How can Mr. David be confident that Michelle will be ready for the work experience? For a student like Michelle, who has a history of disruptive behavior, it will be essential that a behavior plan and other supports be developed and put in place to accommodate her in work experience placements. Michelle is proficient with the computer and enjoys typing her assignments rather than writing them. Mr. David would like to look at a data entry job at the large health insurance company based in their town. But first Mr. David must determine what skills are needed for the jobs chosen by Chris and Michelle.

Assessing Soft Skills for Employment

Mr. David was well aware that in order for either Michelle or Chris to maintain a position in the community, both students needed to have the appropriate soft skills at the worksite. Soft skills include being able to communicate with others, maintaining an appropriate attitude, dressing and acting in a professional manner, working cooperatively with coworkers and supervisors, and being able to think critically and solve problems (Office of Disability Employment Policy, U.S. Department of Labor, June 2012). To gather information about their soft skills, Mr. David investigated the area of formal evaluations by a school psychologist or social worker addressing a student's social skills. He found that one common test that focuses on all levels of adaptive functioning is the Vineland Behavior Scale, Second Edition. Another assessment is the Behavior Assessment System for Children–Second Edition (BASC-2). Mr. David knew that the adaptive scales would be better assessments for determining Michelle's skills in the area of social and interactive skills. Mr. David will need to create supports in order for Michelle to be successful in the employment setting. Social Stories™ can be created to help Michelle deal with situations that may cause outbursts. He also spoke to her parents and discussed the purchase of an iPod for Michelle. Listening to music while working on a computer may minimize her disruptive behavior, and it was determined that there were specific apps to assist with social skills in the work environment. Mr. David found that he could gather information from how Chris interacts socially with others in the classroom and in the community by using informal interviews with teachers and/or with Chris's parents by asking the following questions:

1. Is the student able to state his or her ideas/thoughts clearly?

2. Is the student able to understand and follow directions? What about multistep directions?

3. Is the student able to appropriately accept constructive criticism from his or her peers?

4. Is the student able to appropriately accept constructive criticism from staff?

5. Does the student work well in a team?

6. Is the student able to appropriately ask for help when needed?

7. How does the student handle frustration or stress?

Mr. David thought that he should also administer some informal transition assessments that focus on organization and time management, since these are essential skills needed for college and the world of work. Mr. David could use this information to help identify specific areas of need for Chris within the general areas of organization and time management (see Table 4.2).

ASSESSING THE WORK ENVIRONMENT FOR JOB PLACEMENT

Mr. David knew that he had to understand the work conditions in terms of social interactions (e.g., social norms, many interactions), work production requirements, the actual physical setting, and the environment of the workplace (e.g., fast paced, slow paced), and in order to do so, he had to conduct a community observation and job analysis (see Figure 4.3). Matching students to specific work experiences based on their learning styles

Table 4.2. A sample of informal areas to assess in the areas of organization and time management

Organization	Time management
Assess use of calendar	Assess punctuality
Assess each class for system of organization	Assess time spent engaged in or on activity or task
Assess task completion (turning in assignments)	Assess task completion (turning in assignments)

Community observation

(a) Choose 3–4 different work sites in the mall/community:
(b) Describe the work setting:
(c) Describe the environment: (is it fast paced, standing, moving around)
(d) Describe the informal social interactions and relationships, shared norms, and customs of the environment:

Job analysis

Choose a business in the community (e.g. retail, restaurant, office/clerical work, coffee shop) and analyze how accessible it is for an individual with a specific disability to work in this environment and answer the following questions:

(a) name, address, and phone number of job site,
(b) name of supervisor or significant coworkers,
(c) work hours/days the individual would be working,
(d) a detailed job description,
(e) challenges that might be faced by an individual with this specific disability,
(f) modifications and/or assistive technology that might be necessary in order for an individual with this disability to be successful in this environment,
(g) community services that might be necessary in order for this individual with this disability to have the proper supports in this environment (e.g., bus service),
(h) how willing was this business, in your opinion to work with people with disabilities (e.g., did they seem to welcome individuals with open arms, willing to do whatever is necessary for them to be successful, or did they seem like they would hire someone with a disability if they had to, but would not be very thrilled about it).

Figure 4.3. A sample community observation and job analysis form.

is critical to future job success. One such assessment that Mr. David can consider is the Learning/Working Styles Inventory, which is a component of the Tools for Transition assessment (published by Piney Mountain Press and marketed by Education Associates, Inc.). This learning styles inventory provides voice narration and real-life visuals. This inventory addresses such areas as kinesthetic, visual, tactile, auditory, social, design, light, written, sound, oral, temperature, outdoor/indoor environment, sedentary/nonsedentary, and data/people—all in relation to working styles that are critical for job success.

Mr. David will be able to use this assessment with both Chris and Michelle to match specific work experiences and the strengths of the student to find job matches. The assessment will also provide basic information on supports needed in order for Chris and Michelle to have successful work experiences. Using both the Skills Assessment Module and Tools for Transition will provide information on areas such as motor coordination, finger dexterity, manual dexterity, form/color/spatial perception, following written/oral/diagrammed instructions, and other clerical functions. Mr. David discovered that this specific assessment provided much-needed information on how Michelle and Chris would handle the work environments of the respective career choices they made.

With the strengths and weaknesses of the students identified, Mr. David must now make appointments with specific employers to identify potential work sites. A job analysis requires that Mr. David observe specific job tasks required by the employer and provide a significance ranking to each task. As with all jobs, some tasks are critically important to the job, whereas other tasks may have limited significance. A job analysis provides the functions of a job that are fundamental to the performance level needed. By performing a job analysis, it might be determined that specific work accommodations and/or assistive technology are needed for a successful placement. Assessing the actual job being performed also provides the teacher with the specific details on training that will be needed before the students actually begin their work experiences.

What Kinds of Supports Will the Student Need in Order to Meet the Requirements of This Type of Job?

Mr. David knew that situational assessments (also known as job sampling, on-the-job assessments, or an environmental assessments) assist educators with determining the specific work skills a student has mastered or needs to develop or may not be able to complete. In order to complete situational assessments, Mr. David would have to understand and be able to identify the task for Michelle or Chris to complete at the worksite within the community. In order to evaluate their "job readiness," he would also have to observe the community worksite while Michelle or Chris worked. Without this type of information, Mr. David would not be able to identify the supports needed for either Michelle or Chris (see Table 4.3). Situational assessments should be used to identify the requirements of the job and the student's ability to meet those requirements. To complete the situational assessment, Mr. David shares the responsibility with the district's job coach. Mr. David will contact prospective employers and discuss the length of time required for the situational assessment. The length of the assessment will be dependent on the student involved, as it must be long enough to gather the specific information needed to make a decision about the potential for job placement. In some cases, a situational assessment may take place over several days. During the assessment, information should be documented regarding the requirements of the job and whether the student can perform the job to the level of ability required.

Table 4.3. Areas to be assessed in a situational assessment, as suggested by the Institute on Community Inclusion

• Formality or informality of workplace	• Amount of supervision
• Level of interaction with coworkers/supervisors	• Variety of tasks
• Training required	• Level of worker autonomy
• Stamina and endurance	• Mobility requirements
• Communication	• Production rate
• Strength (lifting and carrying)	• Manual dexterity
• Reading requirements	• Mathematics/counting
• Level of independence required	• Customer contact
• Dress requirements	• Need to work independently
• Flexibility and changes in routine	• Complexity of tasks
• Repetitive nature of tasks	• Amount of self-initiative required
• Need/ability to tell time and time awareness	• Stress and pressure of position
• Need to ask for assistance	• Area orientation requirements
• Environment (noise, temperature, indoors/outdoors)	

Source: National Center on Workforce and Disability (2012).

This type of situational assessment is an example that allows the observer to watch either Michelle or Chris while performing specific job tasks at a potential employment site. Typically, a job coach or employment specialist has the expertise to complete a situational assessment that identifies the requirements of the job, the ability of the students to complete the job, and specific support needs. The job coach can use that information to develop a specific process for teaching Michelle or Chris how to perform the job.

What Are the Resources Available to Support the Transition to Employment?

Mr. David found that each state has programs to assist people with disabilities in the transition to employment. Unlike services provided through the school system under IDEA 2004, adult agency services are based on *eligibility* instead of *entitlement*. Eligibility of services applies not only to qualifying under the guidelines of a particular agency but also to the availability of funding for the services.

Tip: Some state programs require that individuals have Title 19 (Medicaid) in order to receive services. Students may be on their parents' insurance and also have Title 19 insurance. Find out if the agencies in your area require it!

Mr. David also found that each state has a program to assist individuals with disabilities obtain competitive employment. Information can be found on the Rehabilitation Services Administration web site (http://rsa.ed.gov). Mr. David noted that the web site allows you to find the rehabilitation services available in your state.

Additionally, other state agencies that assist with the transition to employment can include the local department or division for developmental disabilities, the department of social services, and the department of mental health. Each state may have different names for these departments as well as different eligibility requirements. Contact the local agencies to understand the steps of the application process.

Mr. David also found out that there are profit and nonprofit companies that provide services for people with disabilities. Services from these companies can be provided through state agencies or obtained through private pay. Mr. David found that an easy way to find a list of companies is either to use the web site of one of the aforementioned state agencies or to contact the local rehabilitation services or department of developmental disabilities to obtain a list of service providers.

IDENTIFYING ASSISTIVE TECHNOLOGY AND OTHER SUPPORTS THAT WILL ALLOW INDIVIDUALS TO PERFORM WORK

After completing the many informal and formal assessments that help target potential employment options, Mr. David knew that both Michelle and Chris may require assistive technology in order to be successful on the worksite. IDEA (2004) covers assistive technology (AT) for students while in the public school setting, but legislation to provide AT in the workplace is not as well delineated. The 1990 Americans with Disabilities Act (ADA; PL 101–336) requires employers with 15 or more employees to provide "reasonable accommodations" for those individuals who self-identify as having a disability. The law provides assistive technology to allow for the employee to perform the essential functions of their job so long as providing the accommodation does not result in an undue hardship to the employer. An undue hardship is defined as a significant expense or challenge associated with implementing the assistive technology device into the existing environment at work. For fear of losing their jobs, many individuals choose not to disclose their disabilities rather than request the needed AT that will allow them to be successful on the job. Job-related AT may be as simple as a color-coordinated flash drive or folder to transfer information or can be as complex as text-to-speech software (*Skills to Pay the Bills*, 2012).

Mr. David knew that he should consider using low-technology methods (e.g., color coding, head phones to handle distractions, and visual schedules) before using high-technology methods (e.g., software programs). Mr. David and the team felt that it was critical to successful employment to monitor the use of the assistive technology with the students. He also understood that if either Michelle or Chris required a technology device, the team would have a hand-written backup just in case the technology malfunctioned, got lost, or needed maintenance.

Mr. David filled out the checklist for Michelle and for Chris in order to determine what, if any, AT or other supports were necessary to assist in their success at the worksite (see Table 4.4). Teachers can utilize the Job Accommodation Network (http://www.askJAN.org) to research assistive technology and accommodation options. This comprehensive web site provides the opportunity to chat live, e-mail, or call a consultant to ask specific questions and guidance. The site provides a sample form that a student would need to complete in order to request an accommodation (see Figure 4.4).

The multidisciplinary team, with input from Chris, determined that he would be able to use his smart phone to assist with his daily work schedule and job tasks and, by using it with headphones, to eliminate distractions. Michelle's AT needs were more

Table 4.4.   A sample checklist for assistive technology and other support

Area	Chris	Michelle
Communication	Portable spell-checker	Augmentative and alternative communication device programmed for specific worksite
Organization	Electronic calendar and task schedule	Visual schedule and timer
Activities of daily living	Medication schedule	None needed
Behavior/attention	None needed	Headphones and iPod

Reasonable Accommodation Request Form for Employers

SAMPLE REASONABLE ACCOMMODATION REQUEST FORM FOR EMPLOYERS

A. Questions to clarify accommodation requested.

What specific accommodation are you requesting?

If you are not sure what accommodation is needed, do you have any   Yes ❑   No ❑
suggestions about what options we can explore?

If *yes*, please explain.

Is your accommodation request time sensitive?   Yes ❑   No ❑

If *yes*, please explain.

B. Questions to document the reason for accommodation request.

What, if any, job function are you having difficulty performing?

What, if any, employment benefit are you having difficulty accessing?

What limitation is interfering with your ability to perform your job or access an employment benefit?

Have you had any accommodations in the past for this same limitation?   Yes ❑   No ❑

If *yes*, what were they and how effective were they?

If you are requesting a specific accommodation, how will that accommodation assist you?

C. Other.

Please provide any additional information that might be useful in processing your accommodation
request:

_____   _____

Signature   Date

Return this form to _____

Figure 4.4. Reasonable accommodation request form for employers.

From Job Accommodation Network (2012). In *Demystifying Transition Assessment*
by Colleen A. Thoma, Ph.D., and Ronald Tamura, Ph.D. (2013, Paul H. Brookes Publishing Co., Inc.)

significant because of the behavioral outbursts. Michelle would be able to use her iPod and headphones to play soft music to block out distracting background noises. Mr. David will develop social stories to help Michelle understand schedule changes, how to communicate appropriately with coworkers, and how to manage her own behavior that may make others around her uncomfortable (Jordan, 2008).

SUMMARY

Mr. David was confident in his ability to develop a plan in the area of employment after going through each step of the process and finding resources that worked for specific students. The Transition Assessment chart at the end of this book provides a listing of transition assessment that he found as he completed his investigation. Did he answer all of the areas and address each area with a type of assessment so that the team could develop an employment profile and be able to support both Michelle and Chris if they were working? The answer is yes—Mr. David revisited the four guiding questions:

1. What job do you want to obtain?

2. What are the requirements for that job in terms of education, experience, social skills (or soft skills), and location?

3. What are the work conditions for this job in terms of social interaction and setting?

4. What kinds of supports will you need in order to meet the requirements of this type of job?

Using a variety of formal, informal, and situational assessments to gather information for Michelle and for Chris, Mr. David felt even more confident that the team would have enough information to develop an appropriate transition plan.

5

Postsecondary Education Assessment

Practices to Document Student Progress, Preferences, and Interests Related to Postsecondary Education and Learning

Joseph W. Madaus, Lyman L. Dukes, III, James E. Martin, and Mary E. Morningstar

Access to postsecondary education has increased significantly for students with disabilities over the past 15 years. For example, in 1978, roughly 3% of all full-time, first-time undergraduates reported a disability (Henderson, 1999). By the 2007–2008 school year, this number had increased to 11% (NCES, 2011). By the same academic year, over 80% of all 2- and 4-year institutions reported serving students with attention-deficit/hyperactivity disorder (ADHD), while 55% of institutions also reported providing services for students with autism spectrum disorders (Raue & Lewis, 2011). So while Mr. David knew that college was a realistic option for Chris and was taking steps in the planning process, he came to realize that college was also a viable option for Michelle. He also understood that planning would need to begin as soon as possible for her. He researched what types of formal and informal assessments might be used in this planning process and how he could involve his students, their families, and his colleagues. But first he had to consider the purpose of transition assessment at the high school level and how this matched up with or differed from the role that assessment might play at the postsecondary level.

PURPOSE OF ASSESSMENT AT THE SECONDARY VERSUS POSTSECONDARY LEVELS

Secondary level. It's important for transition stakeholders to understand that assessment plays a very different role at the secondary and postsecondary levels, partially because of the different policies that outline assessment requirements and purposes. The Individuals with Disabilities Education Act of 2004 mandates a comprehensive and multidisciplinary evaluation before a student can be placed into special education with periodic reevaluations. For students aged 16 and older, such as Michelle and Chris, the law required the use of age-appropriate transition assessments to develop appropriate and measurable postsecondary goals (§300.320[b][1]). This link between assessment and the development of

69

appropriate student goals is clearly articulated in the Division on Career Development and Transition definition of transition assessment (Sitlington, Neubuert, & LeConte, 1997), which states the following:

> Transition assessment is the ongoing process of collecting data on the individual's needs, preferences, and interests as they relate to the demands of current and future working, educational, living, and personal and social environments. Assessment data serve as the common thread in the transition process and form the basis for defining goals and services to be included in the Individualized Education program. (pp. 70–71)

These policy requirements and best practice recommendations from professional organizations and research dictate that transition assessment be an ongoing process that continually tries to capture each student's unique strengths, needs, and preferences (§300.43[a][2]); Sitlington et al., 1997) while being flexible enough to describe current and future work and learning environments (Sitlington et al., 1997). Rojewski (2002) provided a transition assessment model that described three levels of transition assessment, with additional assessments being used for students like Michelle and Chris who are struggling to identify long-term goals and interests. This model can help educators and transition coordinators capture and synthesize existing assessment data, both for the development of Michelle's and Chris's IEPs and for their transition planning, but also for the development of the Summary of Performance (described later in this chapter).

Postsecondary level. At the postsecondary level, assessment is foundational in allowing students to access needed supports and accommodations, but because of different legal mandates, assessment plays different roles with different responsibilities for providing the needed data. At the postsecondary level, institutions are allowed to require objective evidence that verifies and documents that a student has a disability that is current and substantially limits a major life function (Madaus, 2010; U.S. Department of Education, 2007). This evidence is usually referred to as documentation, and it serves two main purposes: to establish that the student should be protected from discrimination on the basis of disability and to determine which accommodations to which the student may be entitled (AHEAD, 2004). Mr. David found a document on the Office for Civil Rights web site titled *Students with Disabilities Preparing for Postsecondary Education: Know Your Rights and Responsibilities* (available online at http://www2.ed.gov/about/offices/list/ocr/transition .html). This document clearly establishes that colleges can require the student to provide this documentation and to assume the cost of any necessary evaluations. In fact, 92% of all postsecondary institutions and 98% of all public 4-year institutions reported requiring such verification of a student's disability (Raue & Lewis, 2011).

Many students with disabilities can use assessment data that was compiled at the secondary level for their postsecondary documentation, but this does not always meet the requirements at different colleges, as each institution can set different standards (Madaus, 2010; Madaus, Banerjee, & Hamblet, 2010). Although secondary schools are not required to assess students to determine eligibility for services in adult agencies or postsecondary settings (IDEA Final Regulations, 2004), some use the "appropriate transition assessments" requirement of the Individuals with Disabilities Education Act (IDEA) to align the assessments used for specific students with the requirements at the postsecondary level (Connecticut State Department of Education, 2009; Madaus et al., 2010). A mix of formal and informal assessment procedures are useful to demonstrate both a student's current level of performance and the functional impact of the disability—in other words, how the disability might interact with the student's learning and the educational requirements of the postsecondary institution (AHEAD, 2004). A description of the types of assessments that can provide information useful to postsecondary educational institutions for a student with ADHD, such as Chris, is provided in the text box about attention-deficit/hyperactivity disorder.

Attention-Deficit/Hyperactivity Disorder

Students requesting accommodations on the basis of ADHD must provide documentation by a professional who has undergone comprehensive training and who has relevant experience in differential diagnosis and the full range of psychiatric disorders (e.g., psychologists, psychiatrists, neuropsychologists, and other relevantly trained medical doctors). The Americans with Disabilities Act Amendments of 2008, which expand major life activities to include "concentrating," will likely render more students diagnosed with this disorder eligible for consideration of accommodations. In addition to the requirements specified in Sections I and II, documentation for students requesting accommodations on the basis of ADHD must include but not be limited to the following:

1. Evidence of early impairment. The condition must have been exhibited in childhood in more than one setting.

2. Evidence of current impairment. A history of the individual's presenting attentional symptoms and evidence of current impulsive/hyperactive or inattentive behaviors that significantly impair functioning in two or more settings must be provided. History of full assessment with current symptoms for past six months.

3. An interview. The interview must contain self-report and third-party information pertaining to: any significant developmental history; family history of ADHD or other educational, learning, physical, or psychological difficulties; relevant medical and medication history; a thorough academic history; and a review of prior psychoeducational test reports to determine whether a pattern of strengths or weaknesses is supportive of attention or learning problems.

4. Description of relevant employment history, or lack thereof.

5. Descriptions of current functional limitations pertaining to an educational setting that are presumably a direct result of problems with attention.

6. Evidence of alternative diagnoses or explanations that have been ruled out. The documentation must investigate and discuss the possibility of alternative or co-morbid mood, behavioral, neurological, learning, and/or personality disorders that may confound the ADHD diagnosis. For a diagnosis of ADHD, the symptoms may not occur exclusively during the course of a Pervasive Developmental Disorder, Schizophrenia, or other Psychotic Disorder, and are not better accounted for by another mental disorder (e.g., Mood Disorder, Anxiety Disorder, Dissociative Disorder, or a Personality Disorder).

7. A discussion of the neuropsychological or psychoeducational assessments administered to determine the current impact of the disorder on the individual's ability to function in an academic setting. Such data should include standard scores, standard deviations, and percentiles reported in table format for those subtests administered.

8. A specific psychiatric diagnosis as per the *Diagnostic and Statistical Manual* of the American Psychiatric Association (2000). Symptoms of hyperactivity/impulsivity which were present in childhood and the current symptoms which have been present for at least the past six months and which impair functioning in two or more settings (e.g., school, work, and home) must also be identified.

(continued)

9. An indication of whether or not the student was evaluated while on medication, and whether or not the prescribed treatment produced a positive response.

10. Prescribed medications, dosages, and schedules that may influence the types of accommodations provided, including any possible side effects.

11. An integrated summary that

    - indicates the substantial limitations to major life activities posed by the disability,
    - describes the extent to which these limitations would impact the academic context for which accommodations are being requested,
    - suggests how the specific effects of the disability may be accommodated, and
    - states how the effects of ADHD are mediated by the recommended accommodations. (From the Connecticut Association on Higher Education and Disability (AHEAD), available at http://www.ahead.org/aff/ctahead/docguidelines.htm#III)

FORMAL ASSESSMENTS

There are multiple formal measures that can be used, and each can have multiple purposes. For example, they might be part of an initial evaluation to determine if a child has a disability and is eligible for special education services, or they might be part of a reevaluation (§300.303) to establish that a student's education program is still appropriate and to determine goals for the next individual education program (IEP). Additionally, the assessments selected can depend on the nature of the student's disability with the goal of answering specific referral questions.

Quite often, such assessments make up the core of documentation presented to the postsecondary institution. The importance of such formal measures in documenting the existence of a learning disability was evidenced in a recent study of college disability service providers (Madaus et al., 2010). Fifty-one percent of college disability service providers require the use of current measures of academic achievement. Moreover, 63% specifically require that these measures be normed on adult populations.

A useful guide to documentation at the postsecondary level from the Connecticut Association on Higher Education and Disability can be found on this organization's web site (http://www.ahead.org/aff/ctahead/docguidelines.htm). The document states that any "assessment, and any resulting diagnosis, should consist of and be based on a comprehensive assessment battery that does not rely on any one test or subtest." It also notes that standard scores should be provided for all normed measures and that the findings should contain an interpretive summary that describes the nature and severity of the disability and describes functional limitations (Connecticut AHEAD, 2008).

The document also lists nine specific disability types (e.g., acquired brain injury; autism spectrum disorder/Asperger syndrome; attention-deficit/hyperactivity disorder; blindness or low vision; deaf or hard of hearing; intellectual disabilities; learning disabilities; disabilities related to physical mobility, dexterity, and chronic health; and psychiatric disorders) and, for each, recommends possible standardized measures that can be used to document the nature of the condition and the impact on student learning.

INFORMAL ASSESSMENTS

Informal assessments are just that: informal. This category of transition assessment includes those that can be bought from educational publishers to assessments that educators and resource center staff make themselves and pass around to their friends and colleagues. These can be paper-and-pencil assessments or structured assessments in community settings that determine students' skills and interests, and they can even include notes from a structured conversation. Like all assessments, informal assessments are useful for some tasks and not for others. Informal assessments cannot, for instance, determine a disability diagnosis or make eligibility decisions. However, as the following examples will demonstrate, results from informal assessments can be used to identify strengths and needs for transition planning discussions.

Mr. David wanted to hold a pre-IEP meeting discussion with Chris and his family about postsecondary education plans. Chris expressed interest in attending a 4-year college, and Mr. David decided to use two informal assessments to frame this discussion. The first assessment helped students and families assess readiness for college. The second assisted in identifying specific nonacademic skills and behaviors needed in order to be successful in postsecondary settings.

Assessing college readiness. Mr. David wanted Chris and his parents to jointly complete *A Guide to Assessing College Readiness* (Landmark College, 2009). Mr. David liked this assessment because it does not examine entrance requirements but instead prompts Chris and his parents to answer a series of "yes" or "no" questions asking about Chris's skill level of behavior pertaining to college success.

This informal paper-and-pencil assessment addresses topics such as academic skills, self-understanding, self-advocacy, executive functioning, and motivation. Items requested that Chris and his parents consider if he 1) has a system for taking notes or can read up to 200 pages a week; 2) can define his disability or identify useful academic supports; 3) can describe his legal rights as a student with ADHD or knows what to do if he is unable to use an appropriate accommodation; 4) has a method to organize and track projects or can complete projects that he finds boring; and 5) knows what he wants to do in 10 years or knows what it will take to be successful in college. If the results indicate a score of fewer than three positive responses in a certain category, the IEP team may want to focus transition goals on that particular category in order to improve his likelihood of postsecondary education success.

Identification of behaviors for postsecondary success. Mr. David also planned to address the results of another assessment in order to help guide the postsecondary education discussion. Mr. David, Chris, and his parents completed a new online transition assessment called the *Transition Assessment and Goal Generator* (TAGG; Martin et al., 2012; available at http://www.ou.edu/content/education/centers-and-partnerships/zarrow/transition-success-assessment-project/educator_trainingmodule.html). Its purpose is to identify strengths and needs relative to nonacademic skills that research has identified as associated with postsecondary education and employment success for former high school students with mild to moderate disabilities. Unlike most informal assessments, several research studies have provided positive validity evidence that supports the use of the TAGG to identify students' strengths and needs relevant to transition and to offer suggestions for annual transition goals.

Each respondent rated how Chris performed in the past year across several categories, including the following: 1) knowledge of strengths and limitations, 2) disability awareness, 3) persistence, 4) proactive involvement, 5) goal setting and attainment, 6) employment, 7) self-advocacy, and 8) use of supports. The TAGG asked Mr. David, Chris, and his parents to indicate if Chris did any of the following: 1) discussed his present level of performance at his IEP meeting and whether he lead his last IEP meeting, 2) distinguished individuals who provided useful support from those who didn't and accepted supports when offered, 3) used a plan to attain his goals and had in fact attained his annual transition goals, 4) successfully participated in small groups to complete projects, 5) continued to work on a goal when it became hard to accomplish, 6) had explained to others the special education services he received, and 7) had accurately shared with others information regarding his academic strengths and challenges. Upon completion, the TAGG provided a computer-generated profile that listed his strengths, needs, and prioritized suggestions for annual transition goals.

Chris, his parents, and Mr. David planned to take the results of the TAGG and the *Guide for Assessing College Readiness* assessments to the next IEP meeting in order to help identify annual transition goals that, when attained, may increase Chris's likelihood for postsecondary success.

Strengths and weaknesses. Informal assessments provide information that secondary educators, students, and family members can use to provide guidance when planning annual and postsecondary goals. These types of assessments cover a wide variety of skills and often target a particular context or situation. Few of these assessments, however, fully disclose how the items were developed or provide adequate validity evidence. This means that educators need to use multiple means to confirm assessment results and verify the results across time—especially if informal assessments are going to be used for transition planning.

Tips for getting the most out of informal assessments. Numerous lists and collections of informal transition assessments exist that educators can use to determine students' strengths and needs as they prepare to transition into postsecondary education. The University of Oklahoma's Zarrow Center (http://zarrowcenter.ou.edu) provides access to several informal assessments. Books such as those written by Gary Clark and his colleagues (Gaumer, Erickson, Clark, and Patton, 2013) or by Robert Miller and his associates (Miller, Lombard, & Corbey, 2007) provide informal transition assessments that can be photocopied and used for multiple purposes. The key in using these assessments is to find a match between what the educator, student, and family need to know and the purpose of the assessment. If available, users should look to determine how the items were developed and if any validity evidence exists, as this information signifies an assessment that has undergone at least some degree of examination in its development. The more rigorous an informal assessment's development and the greater the validity evidence, the better the usability of the results will be. In summary, an informal assessment becomes useful when it fills an instructional need. Even a well-developed assessment with ample validity evidence is worthless if it doesn't meet an instructional need.

ALTERNATE ASSESSMENTS

Sometimes it is not only helpful but also necessary for transition-related professionals to develop and use nonstandardized procedures for assessing student performance. Mr. David understood that standardized assessment methods and even the use of traditional informal assessment measures might not capture all the information needed to help his students achieve their postsecondary goals. He was also aware that, similar to more traditional assessment approaches, such alternate approaches have inherent strengths and limitations. Strengths and limitations for the use of alternate assessment approaches include the following:

Strengths:

- Alternate approaches can be conducted in authentic settings. For example, if social skills are a concern, the student can be observed interacting with classmates or coworkers (Hughes & Carter, 2000).

- Alternate approaches can be classroom assignments and activities already in place. For example, a student's oral presentation or the demonstration of mastery of a particular skill could function as an alternate assessment.

- Alternate assessment measures are inherently flexible and can be individualized based on one's need. For example, a student's collection of materials related to the course subject such as a portfolio.

Limitations:

- As with traditional informal assessment tools, validity and reliability can be a concern.

- In some cases, gathering nontraditional data can be time-consuming. For example, the teacher or transition coordinator may have to develop a tool as well as the instructions for both its use and the interpretation of its results.

Clark (2007) addresses the importance of face validity when using nonstandardized tools for transition planning. The persons using the alternative measure should agree that it have, at a minimum, face validity. This means "the findings are likely to be reasonable for that student and support what is already known about him or her from observations or other data sources" (p. 48). If this is true, Clark suggests that the results of the alternate measure may be considered appropriate for the purposes of transition planning and decision making.

When working with Michelle, Mr. David chose to use a tool he found in his research on the *Think College* web site (http://www.thinkcollege.net). *Think College* promotes postsecondary education options primarily for people with intellectual disabilities. In this case, Mr. David chose to use the *positive personal profile* (PPP; Tilson, n.d.) to better assess Michelle's long-term employability and postsecondary education interests. As Mr. David considered Michelle's lack of clarity about her work and education interests, he determined that the PPP tool would paint a positive and unique picture of Michelle, thus functioning similar to a portfolio but with less emphasis on academic performance. Like a portfolio, it could be used to prepare for job interviews, to guide the development of future IEP goals, and to ensure that both employers and postsecondary education personnel appreciate the individual's strengths and are aware of areas in which the person may need support (Tilson, n.d.). The PPP components, along with sample prompts for each component, are noted in Table 5.1.

Given Chris's interest in pursuing a college education, Mr. David was especially concerned about his ability to use instructional technologies, which are pervasive in today's postsecondary settings. In a 2008–2009 report, the U.S. Department of Labor concluded that ensuring college-bound students have the necessary technology skills was a critical need (McGuire, 2010). The Educational Testing Service defines technologies of this

Table 5.1. Components of the positive personal profile

Profile component	Example prompts
Dreams and goals	How do you picture your life in the future?
Interests	What excites you?
Talents, skills, and knowledge	What are your abilities?
Learning styles	How do you best receive, process, and/or express information?
Values	What do you want out of life?
Positive personality traits	What is special about you?
Environmental preferences	What settings do you prefer?
Dislikes	What would you prefer to avoid?
Life and work experience	What specific skills do you have?
Support system	Who helps you advocate for yourself?
Specific challenges	How does your disability affect you?
Creative solutions/accommodations	In what unique ways can you address your challenges?
Creative possibilities/ideas	Can we brainstorm other ideas to serve you?

From Tilson, G. (n.d.). *Developing a positive personal profile.* Boston: Think College, Institute for Community Inclusion at the University of Massachusetts Boston; adapted by permission.

type as "digital technology, communications tools, and/or networks to access, manage, integrate, evaluate, and create information in order to function in a knowledge society" (2007, p. 2). The broad use of instructional technologies and the rapid adoption of online and hybrid instructional models in college settings means that students with disabilities should be prepared in high school to possess these competencies (Banerjee, 2010).

Given the obvious need to learn and practice using instructional technologies before college, it is vital that this be a part of the transition planning process (McGuire, 2010). Thus, at the outset of Chris's sophomore year, Mr. David, along with Chris's subject area teachers, developed a checklist that will be used to document and evaluate his use of instructional technologies in the classroom. Moreover, as a part of his IEP for the sophomore year, Chris's teachers agreed to document his use of these skills given their importance in college and his interest in college attendance. For example, Chris's social studies teacher assigned students the task of creating the front page of an authentic newspaper from the 1950s. Students were responsible for using primary sources to conduct online research, developing the newspaper layout, writing and editing the newspaper articles, and posting the newspaper on a basic webpage. Following completion of the assignment, the teacher filled out the instructional technologies skills checklist, indicating which skills Chris used, the subject area and assignment name, and his performance level. The instructional skills checklist used by Chris's teacher is provided in the Instructional Technologies Skills Checklist form (see Figure 5.1).

INVOLVING STUDENTS IN POSTSECONDARY ASSESSMENT

Emerging research suggests that active student involvement and leadership in their IEP transition planning process is indicative of postschool employment and educational success (Portley, Martin, & Hennessey, 2012). Students who discuss their transition goals with the IEP team and attain annual transition goals have a much greater likelihood of post–high school success than students who are not actively involved or do not have the opportunity to be involved in the IEP process (Benz, Lindstrom, & Yovanoff, 2000;

Instructional Technologies Skills Checklist

Instructional skill	Course/Assignment	Skill level (H / M / L / NA*)
Reads on the Internet		
Generates search terms / phrases for online searches		
Conducts research using remote access e-databases		
Organizes desktop or hard drive using file management software		
Navigates course management systems such as Blackboard		
Uses e-tools within common word processing programs		
Participates in synchronous and asynchronous online threaded discussions		
Deciphers refereed information from that which is opinion		
Writes research papers using electronic tools and resources		
Uses text, visual, audio, and animation for class projects and presentations		
Uses tools available for tablets and mobile devices		
Uses proper "netiquette"/social network, and e-mail behavior		
Uses electronic calendars		

* H = High skill level / M = Moderate skill level / L = Low skill level / NA = Not applicable

Figure 5.1. Instructional technologies skills checklist. (*Source:* Banerjee, 2010)

Portley et al., 2012). This involvement in transition planning begins with transition assessment. Mr. David, for instance, asked Chris to complete transition assessments, and Chris's results had as much value as those provided by his parents or teachers in determining his transition strengths, needs, and goals. Mr. David also taught Chris what the transition assessment results mean and facilitated a discussion at the IEP meeting in which Chris explained the results of the assessments. Knowing the results enabled Chris to both understand and discuss his strengths and needs as well as to formulate transition goals.

INVOLVING PARENTS IN ASSESSMENT

As Mr. David prepared to assess Michelle and Chris with regard to their future postsecondary educational plans, he considered how he could work as a partner with their families. As a seasoned transition professional, he came to understand that the role of the family is critical when planning for transition to postsecondary education. A good plan will include specific assessment approaches to target the student's postsecondary educational strengths, preferences, interests, and needs while taking into account the influence and support from the student's family. Indeed, there is convincing evidence that the success of a young person's transition to adulthood is often dependent upon long-term support and involvement of the family (Buswell & Sax, 2002). It is particularly important for transition professionals such as Mr. David to understand that both Michelle and Chris's families can offer critical information as well as supports, but these may come at a cost to the family as a whole (Wehmeyer, Morningstar, & Husted, 1999). Considering the family from a systems perspective means that Mr. David will consider both the resources and constraints of the family.

The entire approach shifts from focusing exclusively on the student to including the entire family during the planning and provision of transition services. As with all families, the functions and needs of certain members may take priority over those of other members. To plan for their child's future postsecondary educational goals, parents need to know all possible educational options; however, parents rely on school professionals to provide them with accurate information regarding transition services and outcomes (Wandry & Pleet, 2012). Families are essential in assessing readiness for postsecondary education when they maintain continuity about students' previous transition experiences. For example, Chris's family provided critical information about extra outside tutoring, help with homework, or specific medications and behavioral issues occurring at home. Chris's siblings and extended family members also provided insights about Chris's expectations for postsecondary education and how he interacts outside of parental influence (Morningstar, Wehmeyer, & Dove, 2008). In particular, Chris's parental expectations for postsecondary education will influence attainment of those goals, as parental expectations are a key factor in both academic and career choices and success (Cobb & Alwell, 2009; Wagner, Newman, Cameto, Levine, & Marder, 2007). In fact, parent expectations have been identified as a constant influence on academic achievement both in high school and postsecondary settings for students with and without disabilities, irrespective of mitigating family factors such as parent education level, sex of child, family structure, and amount of family participation (Ma, 1999; Patrikakou, 1996). Transition professionals must also keep in mind that postsecondary expectations may differ between student and his or her parents—as well as between the student/parents and the school (Thompson, Fulk, & Piercy, 2000). This is particularly true for youths and families from culturally and linguistically diverse backgrounds. Beliefs about adulthood, disability, and familial responsibility influence parents' expectations and postsecondary goals for their children with disabilities (Geenen, Powers, & Sells, 2003; Kim & Morningstar, 2005).

For Michelle's family, their limited understanding of the range of postsecondary educational opportunities was a first step in her transition assessment process. This included determining her family's expectations for future postsecondary education and training. Given the emerging research clearly linking higher expectations for academic and career success to positive transition outcomes (Wagner et al., 2007), it was critical that Mr. David work with Michelle's family to fully understand the range of options for possible postsecondary settings. Hanley-Maxwell, Pogoloff, and Whitney-Thomas (1998) advised transition practitioners seeking to build meaningful family involvement in transition planning to first listen to family needs, concerns, opinions, and preferences, including student interests and preferences. Doing so in a manner that supported active participation, such as through effective person-centered planning approaches (Lee, 2010), would be an excellent strategy for fully understanding expectations as well as engaging families.

Person-centered planning not only focuses on the strengths and needs of the student but also empowers families. Kim and Turnbull (2004) defined person-centered planning as an approach that uses family support to engage with community resources. Person-centered planning has also been used to develop collaborative and goal-oriented IEPs (Keyes & Owens-Johnson, 2003). There are a variety of different person-centered approaches (see Table 5.2 for list of resources). A critical element of person-centered planning for Michelle's family was the act of encouraging the family to envision possible postsecondary educational and training options for Michelle and to actively plan to achieve future goals. In addition, providing information about recent developments in supporting youth with intellectual disabilities in postsecondary settings was a positive way to help Michelle's family develop high expectations for postsecondary engagement (Grigal & Deschamps, 2012).

Table 5.2. Resource list for information on person-centered planning

Web sites
Inclusion Press material on PATH, MAPS, and Circles of Friends: http://inclusion.com
Capacity Works by Dr. Beth Mount: http://www.capacityworks.com/index.html
The Person-Centered Planning Education Site: http://www.ilr.cornell.edu/edi/pcp

Materials and workbooks
Building Authentic Visions: How to Support the Focus Person in Person Centered Planning. J. Whitney-Thomas & J. Timmons (1998). Institute for Community Inclusion, Boston, MA. http://www.communityinclusion.org/article.php?article id=31&staff id=42
How to Make Positive Changes for Your Family Member Using Group Action Planning: Group Action Planning as a Strategy for Getting a Life. Beach Center on Disability (n.d.). http://www.beachcenter.org/resource_library/beach_resource_detail_page.aspx?int ResourceID=743&Type=Manual
It's My Choice. W.T. Allen (n.d.). *A self-guided workbook on person-centered planning* published by the Minnesota Governor's Council on Developmental Disabilities. http://www.mnddc.org/extra/publications/choice/Choice1-Intro.pdf
Increasing Person-Centered Thinking: Improving the Quality of Person-Centered Planning: A Manual for Person-Centered Planning Facilitators. A.N. Amado & M. McBride. (2001). Minneapolis: University of Minnesota, Institute on Community Integration. http://rtc.umn.edu/docs/pcpmanual1.pdf.
More Like a Dance: Whole Life Planning for People with Disabilities. Butterworth, J., Hagner, D., Heikkinen, B., Faris, S., DeMello, S., and McDonough, K. (1993). Institute on Community Inclusion, Children's Hospital, Boston. Order from http://www.trninc .com
Planning for Your Transition from High School to Adult Life Workbook. E. Condon & K. Brown (n.d.). The University of Montana Rural Institute http://ruralinstitute.umt.edu/transition/articles.asp
Planning for the Future: A Workbook for Persons with Disabilities, Their Families, and Professionals. M.E. Morningstar (1995). Transition Coalition http://www.transitioncoalition.org

Mr. David used resources such as *Opening Doors to Postsecondary Education* (Kallio & Owens, 2007), which provides information for students and families as well as specific assessment options. This resource offers families information about when to start preparing for postsecondary educational options, differences in laws governing special education and postsecondary education, and questions students and families should ask their IEP team and support networks for postsecondary educational planning. Families, students, and transition professionals can also use the *Postsecondary Education Exploration Worksheet* when they make college visits so as to assess the services, programs, and characteristics of postsecondary settings. Such information is invaluable during the transition assessment and planning process.

COLLABORATION WITH OTHERS IN ASSESSMENT

Mr. David recognized that as the transition coordinator, the responsibility to facilitate the assessment process largely rested with him. But he also appreciated that the most effective "way of work" is to take a collaborative approach to the assessment process. As noted earlier, the determination of a disability and subsequent accommodation decisions in postsecondary environments are intended to provide students with disabilities an equal educational opportunity (Shaw, Dukes, & Madaus, 2012). This means that postsecondary service providers typically prefer to make these decisions after considering a battery of evaluation data, which is typically known as documentation.

In order to provide postsecondary personnel with a rich set of data, Mr. David recognized that it is necessary to enlist the help of numerous disability-related personnel. Therefore, as he prepared to organize the process for assessing Michelle's and Chris's respective interests in and preparation for postsecondary education, he used the information presented in Table 5.3 as a guide for identifying partners who can assist with conducting, interpreting, and reporting assessment data (Clark, 2007). While not intended to be an exhaustive list, Table 5.3 also includes recommendations regarding what information

Table 5.3.   Potential partners in learning assessment

Partner	Potential role
General/special education teachers	Academic achievement evaluation
School administrators	Observational report evaluation
School/behavioral psychologists	Cognitive/behavioral evaluation
School counselors	Postsecondary options evaluation
Paraprofessionals	Classroom data collection
Postsecondary disability personnel	Postsecondary services evaluation
Vocational education personnel	Functional vocational education evaluation
Job coaches/employers	Work-related performance evaluation
School social worker	Social history/social skills evaluation
School nurse	General medical evaluation
Occupational/physical therapists	Fine/gross motor skill evaluation
Speech/language therapists	Speech/language evaluation
Community services personnel	Community services needs/options evaluation
Technology specialists	Assistive technology evaluation
Disability advocacy personnel	Futures planning activities/evaluation

Sources: Clark (2007), Dukes (2010), and Morningstar (2008).

each potential partner might provide. In an ideal situation, when Mr. David was ready to organize the assessment information, the partners would come together face-to-face to discuss these disparate data sources, ensuring that the student be considered holistically rather than in a fragmented manner (Clark, 2007).

With regard to Michelle, Mr. David determined that he would request the participation of a number of important partners. For example, the district assistive technology (AT) specialist provided data regarding the use of her communication device; the teachers from her general education courses and the resource setting in which she participates shared information regarding her academic performance, and the behavioral therapist shared a recently completed functional behavior analysis. Additionally, the vocational education program coordinator was invited to complete a vocational education evaluation to set the stage for more discussion regarding whether this may be an appropriate postsecondary option for Michelle. Ultimately, this data was included in Michelle's Summary of Performance (SOP) portfolio, which was updated annually.

The Summary of Performance

In compliance with the IDEA, Mr. David prepared an SOP—one for Michelle and one for Chris. This tool provides the student and family with one document that, if properly used, effectively condenses a wide range of data relating to the student's unique postsecondary goals (Dukes, 2010). This valuable document provided Mr. David the opportunity to gather the data provided by his assessment partners as well as the opportunity to ensure that postsecondary personnel are provided a comprehensive picture of the student for whom the SOP has been completed (Shaw et al., 2012).

SUMMARY

Postsecondary education is a viable option for many students with disabilities, and effective transition assessment is a critical foundation for the required planning. Ideally, this is a long-term process that begins as early as possible, involves a range of assessment points and types (e.g., formal and informal), and involves a range of participants (e.g., teachers, students, parents, and relevant school professionals). Given the importance of a postsecondary education in today's economy, such careful planning is an essential means to enhance transition planning and to better capitalize on the creativity and productivity of a broad range of students.

6

Health Care Assessment

Edwin Achola, Ronald Tamura, and Cynthia Nixon

Health care transition planning is a purposefully planned process that supports adolescents and young adults with disabilities in their move from pediatric or child-centered to adult-centered health care programs, providers, and facilities (Reiss & Gibson, 2005). The course of health care transition planning process is guided in part by the nature of an individual's medical needs. Some adolescents with disabilities have health care needs that are typical of those of their peers without disabilities who lead relatively healthy lives. Other young adults with disabilities live with chronic health conditions that may require long-term management. Approximately 30% of adolescents experience at least one or more ongoing health condition, such as asthma, cancer, and/or congenital heart disease (Geenen, Powers, & Sells, 2003). Some of these health care concerns may be progressive and affect individuals differently at different periods in time. The varying course and severity of health care needs of Mr. David's students played a significant role in the choices he made regarding determination of appropriate health care assessments and transition activities.

Transition teams face a difficult task in assuring that students with disabilities have access to health care as they transition to adult life. There are a number of factors that define health care transition. According to the 2005–2006 National Survey of Children with Special Health Care Needs, less than half of U.S. youth with special health care needs receive the health care supports and services they need. Since 2005, not much progress has been made toward providing youth with special health care needs with the relevant transition services. The 2009–2010 National Survey of Children with Special Health Care Needs data indicated a slight drop in the proportion of youth with special health care needs who received services necessary to make appropriate transition into adult health care, work, and independence, citing a decrease from 41% in 2005 to 40% (Reiss & Gibson, 2005). These findings are particularly disturbing given that young adults with significant health care needs are more likely than their peers to require long-term health care support. This proportion is even lower among youths who are Hispanic or black and belong to families who are living in poverty or are uninsured or publicly insured (Reiss & Gibson, 2005). Aside from sociodemographic factors such as race and family income, males are even less likely than females to transition successfully. Those without a medical home are at a significant disadvantage. The term *medical home* refers to a model coordinated by a physician that serves as a central source for all medical information and services about the individual. In addition to improving health care outcomes, quality transition services are essential in order to prevent young adults from disengaging with health care services (Watson, 2000).

Another factor to consider when addressing health care transition for youth with disabilities is that of health benefits associated with employment and/or postsecondary education. When looking at movement into adulthood, transition teams need to consider whether the career path chosen is one that will lead to benefits such as health care and life insurance. Many job options that youth with disabilities are placed into will not allow the individual to work sufficient hours to receive such benefits. This, in turn, can limit finding a medical home that will meet the specific needs of the transitioning student. The National Longitudinal Transition Study-2 (Newman, Wagner, Cameto, & Knokey, 2009) reported that only 27% of students working less than 3 years had access to employment-related health insurance, as compared to 51% that had worked between 5 and 8 years. NLTS-2 reported that 32% of students working less than 3 years and 57% of those working more than 5 years had paid sick leave available to them. Disparity existed among disability groups, with 52% of students with learning disabilities as compared to 30% of students with intellectual disabilities or autism having health insurance. Demographics indicated that a higher percentage of those with incomes higher than $25,000 had access to both health insurance and paid sick leave. There was not a significant difference among ethnicities, but attention to gender indicated that males (52%) were more likely to have employment-related health insurance than females (40%). Affordable health insurance outside of the employment setting is difficult, if not impossible, to find, and without health insurance, finding an appropriate physician and medical home can become a very daunting task.

Finally, another factor that the transition team should discuss is the overall wellness of the transitioning student. Educators rarely discuss wellness concerns during a transition planning meeting, especially if those needs are somewhat "invisible." Just as their typical peers, students with disabilities struggle with health issues such as obesity, unhealthy eating habits, lack of sleep, stress, and physical inactivity. Action for Healthy Kids (2011) reports that over 30% of U.S. children are overweight or obese. Overweight children are more likely to become overweight adults. Common knowledge tells us that overweight adolescents can trigger a number of chronic medical conditions, including diabetes, high blood pressure, depression, and sleep disorders. Only 6% of middle and high school students have physical education daily, and 35% of school-age students watch at least 5 hours or more of television on a school day. All of these issues can affect an individual's ability to be productive at work or in a learning environment such as high school or postsecondary education. Mr. David developed a survey to give to Chris, Michelle, and his other students. The *Living A Healthy Life Survey* will allow him to gain valuable information on the lifestyle choices his students are making and how they view their own healthy habits. (See the appendix for information about this and other assessments.)

An appreciation for the dynamic nature of health care needs of young adults is critical in the selection of assessment instruments that can enable planners to anticipate future needs. The changing health care needs encompass all aspects of health, including mental, behavioral, and physical well-being. The centrality of mental and behavioral health cannot be overstated given the potential for stress, and psychological problems at this time are greater for adolescents who have long-term health care needs (While, Forbes, Ullman, Lewis, Mathes, & Griffiths, 2004). Adolescence is a transitional stage during which young adults experience a significant degree of physical and psychological development, and their health care needs evolve nearly as fast. Any planning for health care transition at this stage must account for the expected rapid changes. An important step toward planning for future health care needs requires knowledge of the distinction between adult and pediatric health care systems and of how these different systems can accommodate the evolving health care needs of young adults. Pediatric health care is family focused and developmentally appropriate, and it relies on a significant parental involvement in decision making and prescribes care within a multidisciplinary team (Davis, Rennick, & Majnemer, 2011). Within the adult care system, there is a clear shift in responsibility, decision making, and control from parents to the young adults. With these responsibilities also come rights, such as being able to give consent—including the young adult being able to control access to his or her own medical records. The adult health care system requires autonomy and independent consumer skills, and the depth of family involvement can be significantly reduced. Health care transition assessments should target an assessment of the student's knowledge of the expectations within the adult care system, readiness for additional responsibilities and freedoms, and their preferences related to management of physical well-being. Mr. David realized that he had to learn about the linkages and differences between these two health care systems in order to play a facilitative role in health care transition planning. The complexity of the health care needs—which is furthered by the various systems that a child with a disability might come into contact with and by the number of professionals involved—necessitates a lot of collaboration in health care transition planning.

COLLABORATING WITH OTHERS IN HEALTH CARE ASSESSMENT

The success of the collaborative relationship between parents/guardians, health care professionals, and school personnel in supporting a learner's path to independence depends on prioritizing developmentally appropriate concerns of adolescents. Blum, Garell, and Hodgman (1993) and Pywell (2010) suggested that a shift of focus to parents poses the danger of neglecting critical adolescent issues such as sexual and reproductive health care, substance abuse, a healthy diet, regular exercise, dental hygiene, vocational counseling, and independent living. The web of individuals supporting the adolescent's health care transition needs works best when a central person manages communication between health care professionals, parents/guardians, the student, relevant agencies, and school personnel. The coordinator is usually a professional from the child health care team who has had ongoing involvement with that student or is someone from the adult service who will be involved in the future. This individual should be chosen in consultation with the student (Pywell, 2010). Involving the student in the selection of the coordinator not only gives him or her an opportunity to exercise self-determination; it also indicates to the student that his or her opinions and contributions are valued. After all, it is the student's transition to adulthood that is being planned.

Mr. David realized that the value of each stakeholder playing his or her part effectively was immeasurable. To ensure that everybody played their parts, he began by understanding the roles and concerns of each of the participants in the transition planning process. Geenen et al. (2003) indicated that health care providers were most helpful in the following areas:

1. Assisting adolescents and their families in understanding how an adolescent's health condition and disability may affect employment or postsecondary education

2. Helping the student gain the knowledge and skills necessary to communicate with others about his or her condition and advocate for necessary accommodations

3. Helping the youth identify appropriate accommodations

Geenen at al. (2003) further suggested that some of the barriers to successfully participating in the transition process that are faced by health care providers include lack of time, feeling uncomfortable discussing certain issues with youth, inadequate expertise in transition planning, and lack of sufficient information from families.

Involving the School in Health Care Transition

The school system plays a vital role in teaching students to live healthy lives that will prevent future medical conditions that hinder their learning and employment. The first step is to visit the district office and meet with the individuals that coordinate services impacting nutrition, physical education, and health education classes. One way to ensure collaboration between the education team and health professionals is to investigate forming a school wellness committee that can research the health initiatives within the district. While most high schools only offer one credit of physical education during a student's high school tenure, Mr. David plans to seek out ways to provide daily physical activity and fitness for all students. One specific idea is an after-school club focusing on these issues. For example, Mr. David would like to start a walking club, and he would like to partner with local businesses as sponsors willing to provide student prizes based on the number of miles walked. All students in his high school would be invited to participate. Working with the physical education teacher to address any health concerns of specific students, students can set appropriate goals to achieve specific, tangible rewards. Finally, Mr. David plans to meet with the coordinator for the school lunch program and look at ways to improve the nutritional value of food options offered to high school students at lunch. By assessing the health wellness of his students, Mr. David believes that he can help prevent chronic health problems for the future.

Involving Parents in Health Care Transition

Parental involvement is critical in the health care transition process as learners begin making strides toward making informed decisions independently. Parents can be very helpful in conducting assessments, implementing transition plans, and evaluating the success of these plans. The transition process should not only focus on the direct health care needs of the learners; parental concerns also need to be factored in (Davis et al., 2011). Informal discussions provide a good avenue for understanding parental concerns about their children's transition needs. Some of the transition activities parents consider most important include coordinating the child's health with other health care professionals, helping the child to get health insurance, finding an adult health care provider when the child becomes an adult, teaching the child how to manage his or her own heath, and working with the school to coordinate care (Geenen at al., 2003). This list can provide a good starting point in identifying ways that parents can contribute to their child's successful transition to adult life.

Parents, however, feel they have very little preparation for the eventual transition from the pediatric system to the adult health care setting. Davis et al. (2011) suggested that parents are fearful of the unknown in relation to the availability of appropriate services to address the multifaceted needs of not only the young adult but also the needs of the family. The trusting relationship developed with the pediatric system over time does not automatically carry over into the adult system. Mr. David therefore needed to incorporate parent education as part of the overall transition planning process, including facilitating informal parental support networks. These networks would link parents of the transitioning youth with other parents, teachers, and friends whose children had been through the process. Nonetheless, parents and young adults must be weaned away from previous existing relationships and routines within the pediatric system in order to build new ones (Rapley & Davidson, 2009). It is, however, important to keep in mind that parental involvement needs to be gradually minimized as the youth becomes more independent.

The implications of health care transition planning extend beyond facilitating an individual's transition into the adult care system. Health care concerns also affect other transition domains, including employment, independent living, and postsecondary education (Geenen et al., 2003). A student may need special housing arrangements at college as well as a host of other accommodations in classes due to health care needs. While planning for postsecondary education, such a learner would need to have conversations with college officials to explore the possibility of obtaining relevant accommodations in a timely fashion.

One possible side effect of the antianxiety medication that Chris takes is the possibility of developing slurred speech and double vision. As part of his goal to transition to college, his health care transition team developed a plan to help Chris identify some of the possible side effects of the medication and which ones required immediate medical attention versus those that were less serious and thus able to be discussed with his health care provider at his next appointment. A second part of Chris's plan was learning to make decisions about whether and how to disclose these challenges to his professors and close peers. Disclosing these health concerns could be helpful in advocating for accommodations such as flexible schedules and in identifying peers who could possibly serve as back-up support to help with monitoring the effects of his medication.

ASSESSMENTS

The purpose of a transition readiness assessment for health care is to identify stakeholder interests, preferences, support needs, and targets for intervention so as to enhance the likelihood of successful engagement with adult oriented care—and to measure improvement in transition over time (Schwartz, Tuchman, Hobbie, & Ginsberg, 2011). The majority of health care transition assessments are nonstandardized measures or checklists that provide a foundation for the development of transition plans. Health care transition plans should, at the very least, clearly spell out the main concerns of the student and other stakeholders, information on the student's current level of performance, plans for interventions, persons responsible for each plan, and time frames for achievement and review. A logical starting point is the gathering of information about a student's self-advocacy skills, independent health care behavior, sexual health, psychosocial support, postschool plans, and general lifestyle. Typically, these informal assessments rely on students to self-report, and while these assessments have been found to be useful, one must keep in mind their inherent weaknesses (Mittal, Ahern, Flaster, Maesaka, & Fishbane, 2001). Most people believe that they have a lower than average risk of developing health complications, regardless of the actual risk, and adolescents have an even greater tendency to believe they are invincible (Dunning, Heath, & Suls, 2005). Some amount of caution is therefore required in using such measures with young adults, who are also at a significant risk of failing to engage with health services or comply with treatment (Watson, 2000).

Given the variability of health care transition needs of youth, Mr. David realized that having each transition team selecting specific assessments/measures for readiness was quite helpful. Some generic transition checklists have been developed as alternatives to the readiness measures (Kennedy, Sloman, Douglass, & Sawyer, 2007); these measures and checklists include the following:

- *Health Care Transition Transfer of Care Checklist (Young Adult)*

- *Health and Wellness Skills*

- *Health and Wellness 101: The Basic Skills*

- *STARx Questionnaire*

- *Your Child's Heath Care Independence Worksheet 2 for Parents of Youth Ages 12–14*

- *Parent's Health Care Transition Activities*

- *Thinking About Your Future*

- *Now That You Are Eighteen: Young Adult Transition Plan Worksheet*

Some of these measures have both youth and parent versions. Mr. David found that obtaining responses from both the student and parents built a platform from which conversations about health care transition could take place. Parents and their children compared their responses and worked together to begin identifying activities that the student could do independently while exploring those that required more work. After building consensus on areas of need, the transition team uses this information to develop both short- and long-term transition goals and activities the youth will engage in to reach these goals. Mr. David administered the Health and Wellness 101: Basic Skills assessment to both Chris and his mom. Even though Health and Wellness 101: Basic Skills is designed for the student, it can also be adapted for family members who are knowledgeable about the learner's current level of performance. Results from this measure indicated both points of convergence and transition issues that Chris and his parents needed to agree on. See Figures 6.1 and 6.2.

From this measure, it was clear that Chris and his mom took similar positions regarding his ability to explain to others how their family's customs and beliefs might affect the following: health care decisions and medical treatments, his baseline knowledge of health and wellness baseline, his knowledge of symptoms that need quick medical attention, response to medical emergency, preparation before a doctor's appointment, his role in filling medical records, his role in giving consent, monitoring medical equipment, and future health insurance plans. However, it became apparent that Chris and his mom had divergent opinions regarding the following: Chris's understanding of his health care needs and disability, whether he carries his insurance card, and his role in doctors' appointments and getting prescriptions refilled.

In the discussion about the results of the assessment, Mr. David facilitated the synchronization of the divergent perspectives taken by Chris and his mom in order to develop realistic health care transition goals. In fifth grade, after bouts of coughs and chest tightness, Chris was diagnosed with asthma. This has since been effectively controlled with step down therapy and occasional use of albuterol. While Chris believes he understands his health care needs and disability and can explain these needs to others, his mom was convinced that he does not fully understand the impact of his asthma. It was agreed that Chris would begin monitoring and keeping track of the environments in which he experiences symptoms of asthma attack so as to help identify environmental triggers. Such self-monitoring strategies would help him prevent attacks in new settings—especially now

Transition Readiness Changing Roles for Youth

Compare your answers with your family. They might be surprised what you know or what you want to learn. Work on a plan to increase your health care skills. Share with the medical team the skills that you are working on. It takes time and practice to learn and demonstrate these skills. Best time to start, is today!

Chris

Health & Wellness 101 The Basic Skills	Yes, I do this	I want to do this	I need to learn how	Someone else will have to do this - Who?
KNOWLEDGE OF HEALTH ISSUES/DIAGNOSIS				
1. I understand my health care needs, and disability and can explain my needs to others.	✓			
2. I can explain to others how our family's customs and beliefs might affect health care decisions and medical treatments.			✓	
3. I know my health and wellness baseline (pulse, respiration rate, elimination habits)			✓	
4. I know my symptoms that need quick medical attention.	✓			
5. I know what to do in case I have a medical emergency	✓			
BEING PREPARED				
6. I carry my health insurance card everyday	✓			
7. I carry my important health information with me every day (i.e., medical summary, including medical diagnosis, list of medications, allergy info., doctor's numbers, drug store number, etc.)		✓		
TAKING CHARGE				
8. I call for my own doctor appointments.		✓		
9. I know I have an option to see my doctor by myself.		✓		
10. Before a doctor's appointment I prepare written questions to ask.			✓	
11. I track my own appointments and prescription refills expiration dates.				My mom
12. I call in my own prescriptions refills.				My mom
13. I have a part in filing my medical records and receipts at home.			✓	
14. I pay my co-pays for medical visits.				My parents
15. I co-sign the "permission for medical treatment" form (with or without signature stamp, or can direct others to do so).			✓	
16. I help monitor my medical equipment so it's in good working condition (daily and routine maintenance).	✓			
AFTER AGE 18				
17. My family and I have a plan so I can keep my healthcare insurance after I turn 18 and 26.		✓		
18. I sign my own medical forms (HIPAA, permission for treatment, release of records)		✓		
19. My family and I have discussed and plan to develop a legal Power of Attorney for health care decisions in the event my health changes and I am unable to make decisions for myself. (Everyone in the family should have one!)		✓		

Figure 6.1. Chris's completion of "Transition Readiness: Changing Roles for Youth." (You are welcome to use this tool, Changing Roles, as is or adapt it to your setting or needs. © Got Transition™. The National Health Care Transition Center is a program of the Center for Medical Home Improvement™, funded through a cooperative agreement [U39MC18176] from the U.S. Maternal and Child Health Bureau, HRSA, DHHS. This tool was adapted from the federally funded HRSA/MCHB HRTW Tool, Changing Roles, developed by Patti Hackett, Ceci Shapland, and Mallory Cyr [2006, 2009]. Revised 2011 by Patti Hackett, M.Ed.)

Transition Readiness: Changing Roles for Youth

Compare your answers with your family. They might be surprised what you know or what you want to learn. Work on a plan to increase your health care skills. Share with the medical team the skills that you are working on. It takes time and practice to learn and demonstrate these skills. Best time to start is today!

Chris

Health & Wellness 101 The Basic Skills	Yes, I do this	I want to do this	I need to learn how	Someone else will have to do this - Who?
KNOWLEDGE OF HEALTH ISSUES/DIAGNOSIS				
1. I understand my health care needs, and disability and can explain my needs to others.			✓	
2. I can explain to others how our family's customs and beliefs might affect health care decisions and medical treatments.			✓	
3. I know my health and wellness baseline (pulse, respiration rate, elimination habits)			✓	
4. I know my symptoms that need quick medical attention.	✓			
5. I know what to do in case I have a medical emergency	✓			
BEING PREPARED				
6. I carry my health insurance card everyday			✓	
7. I carry my important health information with me every day (i.e., medical summary, including medical diagnosis, list of medications, allergy info., doctor's numbers, drug store number, etc.)			✓	
TAKING CHARGE				
8. I call for my own doctor appointments.			✓	
9. I know I have an option to see my doctor by myself.			Doesn't know	
10. Before a doctor's appointment I prepare written questions to ask.			✓	
11. I track my own appointments and prescription refills expiration dates.			Needs to learn	
12. I call in my own prescriptions refills.			Needs to learn	
13. I have a part in filing my medical records and receipts at home.			Needs to learn	
14. I pay my co-pays for medical visits.				Parents
15. I co-sign the "permission for medical treatment" form (with or without signature stamp, or can direct others to do so).			Needs to learn	
16. I help monitor my medical equipment so it's in good working condition (daily and routine maintenance).	✓			
AFTER AGE 18				
17. My family and I have a plan so I can keep my healthcare insurance after I turn 18 and 26.		✓		
18. I sign my own medical forms (HIPAA, permission for treatment, release of records)		✓		
19. My family and I have discussed and plan to develop a legal Power of Attorney for health care decisions in the event my health changes and I am unable to make decisions for myself. (Everyone in the family should have one!)		✓		

Figure 6.2. Chris's mom's completion of "Transition Readiness: Changing Roles for Youth." (You are welcome to use this tool, Changing Roles, as is or adapt it to your setting or needs. © Got Transition™. The National Health Care Transition Center is a program of the Center for Medical Home Improvement™, funded through a cooperative agreement [U39MC18176] from the U.S. Maternal and Child Health Bureau, HRSA, DHHS. This tool was adapted from the federally funded HRSA/MCHB HRTW Tool, Changing Roles, developed by Patti Hackett, Ceci Shapland, and Mallory Cyr [2006, 2009]. Revised 2011 by Patti Hackett, M.Ed.)

that he anticipates moving away from home. It was also agreed that with the help of his mom and Mr. David, Chris would develop his own Google calendar (see Figure 6.3) with reminders about doctors' appointments and dates to refill prescriptions.

His mom also learned that although Chris carries his insurance card in his wallet, he often forgets to bring his wallet along with him when he is leaving the house. In order to help Chris remember, on his Google calendar each day there is a reminder to bring his wallet before leaving the house. When asked about how he would be able to consult effectively with his doctor during visits, Chris suggested that he would keep a journal detailing some of his health concerns to help him remember what to ask the doctor. Chris would also use information from the same journal to fill in his medical records back at home. Mr. David also decided that using a decision tree that would help identify areas of strength and areas of concern for medication and health care needs. In this example, a decision tree would include steps that Chris would follow in order to ensure that he was taking his prescribed medication (see Figure 6.4).

One of the health care transition measures that Michelle's transition team selected was *Your Child's Health Care Independence Worksheet 2 for Parents of Youth Age 15–17* (see Figure 6.5). This measure includes both the student and parent versions. Results from this assessment indicated that Michelle is able to take her medication correctly, tell when her medical supplies are low, take care of her medical equipment, tell when the equipment has problems, let her doctors and nurses know what's wrong, and spend time with the doctor alone during health care visits. In the health care transition plan, these tasks were listed as mastered skills that she could already accomplish independently. The team learned that

Chris's Calendar						
MAY 2012				Week	Month	Agenda
Sun	Mon	Tue	Wed	Thu	Fri	Sat
30	May 1	2	3	4	5	6
10 am Math Tutoring				12 pm Lunch with Bill	10 am Class	
7	8	9	10	11	12	13
10 am Math Tutoring			11 am Class	12 pm Dental appointment		
14	15	16	17	18	19	20
10 am Math Tutoring				12 pm Trip to the zoo		
21	22	23	24	25	26	27
10 am Math Tutoring						
28	29	30	31	June 1	2	3
Prescription refill					Volunteers meeting	

Figure 6.3. Chris's calendar.

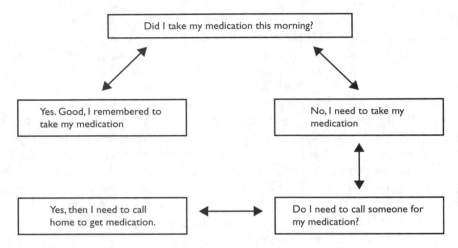

Figure 6.4. A sample decision tree.

she has trouble, however, making good choices about food, friends, exercise, alcohol, and smoking in order to stay healthy. It was also clear that Michelle had difficulty keeping track of the medical tests and appointments to which she regularly goes.

The team agreed that Michelle would work together with a nutritionist in developing a healthy meal plan and learning more about healthy food. Michelle indicated that she enjoyed getting groceries and cooking together with her dad, so the team agreed to use this opportunity to reinforce lessons about preparing nutrient-rich foods and making healthy decisions about portion sizes. Having participated in a social skills program last summer at the local YMCA, which was an activity she really enjoyed, the team agreed that Michelle would try out an after-school program at the same place. This prospect would afford her additional socialization opportunities and a customized exercise regimen to help her with weight management. Michelle would also begin, together with her sister's help, using a large calendar at home to help her keep track of appointments and her daily schedule.

Finally, Mr. David knew that he should include a situational assessment such as the Repertoire Charts (see Figure 6.6) that he could administer and then use to look at the level performance and critical features that could be used for both Michelle and Chris. This type of checklist rating scale identifies the level of assistance needed in to perform skills in the areas of hygiene and toileting and safety and health. Mr. David would have to observe both Michelle and Chris engaging in the routines associated with the checklist so that accurate measurements could be recorded.

The process of getting young people involved in developing health care transition plans is an important step toward responding to their increasing need for self-determination and autonomy. The responsibility for decision making should be increased gradually, and the process should be discussed and accompanied by formal documentation of clinical care, needs assessment, and interagency agreement. Wherever possible, these documents, in the form of hand-held records, should be accessible to the young person (Maynard, De Sousa, Needham, Smith, & McDonagh, 2004). Availing these documents should enable the student to be able to perform reasonable self-assessment in response to the self-report measures typically used in health care transition planning. The process of making self-assessment also affords learners an opportunity to ask questions, gather more information,

Your Child's Health Care Independence:
Worksheet 2 for Parents of Youth Ages 15–17

Instructions

Please rate your child's ability to carry out each of the following health care activities by placing an X in the column that best describes her/his behavior. If an item does not apply, put "NA" in the first column.

	Basic Knowledge	My child does this independently OR knows how to do this and directs others	My child does this with some help	My child cannot do this OR does this only with lots of help
1.	My child can tell someone what her/his diagnosis, disability or health condition is.			✓
2.	My child can describe her/his disability or health condition and its affect on her/his body			✓
3.	My child can describe how her/his disability or health condition effects her/his daily life			✓
4.	My child can tell a doctor or nurse her/his medical history			✓
5.	My child can tell someone about the health problems her/his disability or health condition often causes.			✓
6.	My child can list her/his allergies and get help when she/he has an allergic reaction.		✓	
7.	My child keeps a personal health notebook or medical journal			✓
8.	My child carries a Medical Summary (a written form that has information about her/his diagnosis, medications, equipment, doctors, and what to do in a medical emergency.)	✓		

Health Care Transition Worksheets for Parents of Youth, Ages 15-17

	Health Care Practices	My child does this independently OR knows how to do this and directs others	My child does this with some help	My child cannot do this OR does this only with lots of help
1.	My child dresses, feeds, bathes, and care for her/himself		✓	
2	My child completes daily or usual medical tasks		✓	
	List usual or daily medical tasks & rate your child's independence			
a.				
b.				
c.				
d.				
3.	My child can tell someone what smoking, taking drugs or alcohol, or the lack of exercise can do to her/him			✓
4.	My child makes good choices about friends, food, exercise, alcohol and smoking in order to stay healthy			✓
5.	My child does a Testicular Self Exam or Breast Self Exam regularly			✓
6.	My child knows about abstinence until marriage, safe sex practices, birth control and how to protect her/himself against STD's			✓
7.	My child can tell someone about how her/his disability or health condition might effect her/his sexual development and reproductive health			✓

Health Care Transition Worksheets for Parents of Youth, Ages 15-17

(continued)

Figure 6.5.   Your child's health care independence: Worksheet 2 for parents of youth ages 15–17. (From Reiss, J. & Gibson, R. [2005]. *Health care transition workbook.* Gainesville, FL: Institute for Child Health Policy at the University of Florida.)

Figure 6.5. *(continued)*

	Medications, Medical Tests, Equipment and Supplies	My child does this independently OR knows how to do this and directs others	My child does this with some help	My child cannot do this OR does this only with lots of help
1.	My child can name her/his medications (using their proper names), and the amount and times she/he takes them			✓
2.	My child can tell someone why she/he takes each of her/his medications		✓	
3.	My child can tell someone what the side effects of her/his medications are		✓	
4.	My child takes her/his medications correctly	✓		
5.	My child can tell someone the difference between generic and brand name (proprietary) medications			✓
6.	My child selects the medications she/he needs when she/he has a minor illness (a headache or a cold)	✓	✓	
7.	My child can tell someone about medications that should not be taken because they might interact with her/his medications		✓	
8.	My child can tell someone what happens if she/he does not take her/his medication correctly		✓	
9.	My child tells me when her/his supply of medications is low, and orders more		✓	
10.	My child can list the medical tests she/he has regularly and makes sure these are done on time		✓	
11.	My child uses and takes care of her/his medical equipment and/or supplies; contacts vendors about equipment problems and/or orders her/his supplies when they are running out		✓	

Health Care Transition Worksheets for Parents of Youth, Ages 15-17

	Doctor Visits	My child does this independently OR knows how to do this and directs others	My child does this with some help	My child cannot do this OR does this only with lots of help
1.	My child tells her/his doctors and nurses what's wrong	✓		
2.	My child answers many of the questions during a health care visit		✓	
3.	My child asks many questions during a health care visit		✓	
4.	My child fills out her/his personal health history form at the doctor's office			✓
5.	My child spends most of the time alone with the doctor(s) during health care visits	✓		
6.	My child, her/his doctors and I decide together what medicines and treatments she/he needs	✓		
7.	My child can contact her/his doctors to tell them about unusual changes in her/his health.			✓
8.	My child tells her/his doctors that she/he understands and agrees with the medicines and treatments they suggest	✓		

Health Care Transition Worksheets for Parents of Youth, Ages 15-17

	Health Care Transition	My child has done this	My child has NOT done this
1.	My child has found out from her/his doctors if they stop seeing patients at a certain age (for example, if they do not take care of patients who are older than 21)		✓
2.	My child has talked with her/his doctor or nurse about going to different doctors when she/he is an adult		✓
3.	My child has talked with doctors and family about what things to consider when selecting adult doctors (for example: size of the practice, experience with taking care of people with her/his condition or disability)		✓
4.	My child has helped to identify some adult doctors that she/he might go to when she/he is older		✓
5.	My child has set goals for taking care of her/his own health		✓
6.	My child has taken more responsibility for her/his own health care by learning new skills	✓	
7.	My child has talked to older kids or young adults about health care transition		✓
8.	My child has talked with her/his nurse or social worker about health care transition		✓

Health Care Transition Worksheets for Parents of Youth, Ages 15-17

	Health Care Systems	My child does this independently OR knows how to do this and directs others	My child does this with some help	My child cannot do this OR does this only with lots of help
1.	My child can tell someone the date and reason for her/his next health care appointment		✓	
2.	My child can call her/his primary care doctor's or specialist's office to make or change an appointment			✓
3.	My child can tell someone the name of her/his health insurance plan		✓	
4.	My child can tell someone how her/his health insurance works (co-pays, deductibles, provider networks)			✓
5.	My child can tell someone about limitations that her/his health insurance plan has and problems she/he need to watch out for when ordering supplies and/or medication and other equipment			✓
6.	My child can tell someone if she/he receives benefits from the Supplemental Security Income (SSI) Program and if she/he might be eligible for SSI when she/he turns 18			✓
7.	My child can tell someone the differences between a primary care doctor and a specialist			✓
8.	My child can tell someone what adult doctors expect their patients to be able to do (meet with them alone, answer and ask questions, make decisions about their health care)		✓	
9.	My child can tell someone what new legal rights and responsibilities she/he will have when she/he turns 18 (for example, sign medical consent forms and make medical decisions)			✓
10.	My child can tell someone how long she/he can be covered under the family health insurance plan, and what she/he needs to do to maintain coverage (such as be a full time student)			✓

Health Care Transition Worksheets for Parents of Youth, Ages 15-17

Repertoire Charts

Goal area	Present activities	Performance level			Has related social skills?	Critical features			Note priority goal areas
		Check all				Check one that apply			
		Assistance on most steps	Assistance on some steps	Independent		Initials as needed?	Makes choices?	Uses safety measures?	
Hygiene and toileting	Use public and private toilets								
	Wash hands and face: routine times and for specific activities (food preparation)								
	Follow acceptable hygiene practices								
	Manage menstrual care								
Safety and health	Follow safety rules								
	Exit building for emergency/alarm								
	Take care with utensils, appliances, and tools								
	Inform other(s) when sick/injured								
	Take medicine as needed								

Figure 6.6. Repertoire Charts.

From Ford, A., Schnorr, R., Meyer, L.H., Davern, L.A., Black, J., & Dempsey, P. (1989). *The Syracuse community-referenced curriculum guide for students with moderate and severe disabilities* (pp. 377–378). Baltimore, MD: Paul H. Brookes Publishing Co.; reprinted by permission. In *Demystifying Transition Assessment* by Colleen A. Thoma, Ph.D., and Ronald Tamura, Ph.D. (2013 by Paul H. Brookes Publishing Co., Inc.)

Repertoire Charts (continued)

Goal area	Present activities	Performance level — Check all			Has related social skills?	Critical features — Check one that apply			Note priority goal areas
		Assistance on most steps	Assistance on some steps	Independent		Initials as needed?	Makes choices?	Uses safety measures?	
Safety and health (Continued)	Avoid/report sexual abuse								
	Report emergencies								
	Use caution with strangers								
	Use phone to obtain emergency help								
	Avoid alcohol and other drugs								
	Know appropriate first-aid procedures: minor, major incidents (choking, bleeding, artificial respiration)								
	Maintain good personal health habits								
	Manage birth control as needed								
Assisting and taking care of others (examples)									

From Ford, A., Schnorr, R., Meyer, L.H., Davern, L.A., Black, J., & Dempsey, P. (1989). *The Syracuse community-referenced curriculum guide for students with moderate and severe disabilities* (pp. 377–378). Baltimore, MD: Paul H. Brookes Publishing Co.; reprinted by permission. In *Demystifying Transition Assessment* by Colleen A. Thoma, Ph.D., and Ronald Tamura, Ph.D. (2013 by Paul H. Brookes Publishing Co., Inc.)

and begin setting goals. Such avenues for asking questions create a window of opportunity to discuss subjects that can be sensitive, such as matters related to sexual health.

APPLYING THE PRINCIPLES OF UNIVERSAL DESIGN FOR LEARNING (UDL) TO HEALTH CARE ASSESSMENT

An abundance of elements of universal design for learning (UDL) abound in the health care assessment procedures currently in use. UDL is not a set method of instruction but rather a framework for instructional design that is built on the principle that all students can learn (Thoma, Bartholomew, & Scott, 2009). Most of the health care checklists are designed as pencil-and-paper measures, while others can be responded to on computers. Having both options available provides alternative avenues for learner engagement and expression, thereby allowing them to select assessment modes they are most comfortable with. Other pertinent health care transition information can be gathered through informal interviews and by engaging both parents and health care professionals. Multiple sources of information provide a holistic picture of the needs, preferences, strengths, and interests of the young adult.

SUMMARY

Consider the following important facts:

- Every year, an estimated 750,000 adolescents between the ages of 15 and 19 become pregnant (American College of Obstetricians and Gynecologists, 2012).

- Approximately 46% of females and of males report ever smoking at least one cigarette, with 19% of females and 20% of males having smoked in the past month (Centers for Disease Control and Prevention, 2012).

- An estimated 12.5% of children and adolescents between the ages of 6 and 19 have suffered permanent damage to their hearing from excessive exposure to noise (Centers for Disease Control and Prevention, 2012).

- In 2008, more than one third of children and adolescents were overweight or obese (Centers for Disease Control and Prevention, 2012).

- Approximately 85% of all adolescents are mildly sleep deprived, and 10–40% may be significantly sleep deprived (Bergin & Bergin, 2010).

- More than 70% of students report that they often or always feel stressed by their schoolwork, with 61% of students reporting that schoolwork/homework frequently keeps them from other things, such as spending time with family and friends (Conner, Pope, & Galloway, 2010).

For students with disabilities, the ability to manage their own wellness and health care needs should be a fundamental part of every transition plan. The facts provided above all have consequences that affect learning and employment, which often leads to increased medical care, absenteeism from school or work, and psychological and/or social problems. In a recent study, the research confirmed that significant barriers to considering health care transition included lack of awareness and knowledge by the stakeholders and the perception that health care was a low priority. The implications from the research are clear and necessary. A three-prong approach needs to be adopted by school districts and should include the following: 1) a school-based curriculum to address health care needs,

2) district guidelines to provide for the inclusion of health and medical information in transition plans, and 3) the inclusion of medical and/or health personnel in the transition process (Repetto, Gibson, Lubbers, Gritz & Reiss, 2008). Clearly this requires a systems change for states and districts. Educators need to be trained to assess health care and wellness needs of all students with disabilities—even those who appear to be healthy and fit. Health wellness and care is not just for students with disabilities; it is for all students. In the long run, the benefits are immeasurable. Healthy adults can translate into productive citizens.

FOR FURTHER INFORMATION

	Type of Resource	Links
Forms	Health history forms Health skills checklists Health care transition planning guides Other tools	http://depts.washington.edu/healthtr/resources/tools.html
Audio/visual	Tools	http://hctransitions.ichp.ufl.edu/products_videos.php
Support groups	Self Advocates Becoming Empowered (SABE) Kids As Self Advocates (KASA)	http://www.sabeusa.org http://fvkasa.org/index.php

7

Community Assessment

Christina C. Bartholomew and Colleen A. Thoma

Community involvement has long been considered an important component of transition planning for students with disabilities. However, planning for community involvement can sometimes be a struggle for teachers, as they must consider the students' abilities, needs, and interests as well as identify and develop meaningful collaborative opportunities with partners in the community. To effectively accomplish this, teachers and/or transition coordinators need a systematic assessment plan that examines potential community partners as well as a plan that effectively collects assessment data on students prior to, during, and after community experiences so that they can develop an accurate picture of the students' interests, abilities, and growth. Members of the transition planning team should consider the following questions: What opportunities are available in our community for students to be a part of now, and how can I create a variety of experiences for all of my students? How can I assess students' abilities, interests, and support needs in order to help them create and accomplish their goals in the community? How can I collect data while engaged in community activities that will be useful in continuing to create meaningful transition opportunities?

Chris

As Chris continued on his path in transition he struggled with understanding how he could become involved in the community or the types of things in which he might want to be involved. He knew that he would have to make some decisions about employment and education, but it was hard for him to begin thinking about how and where in the community he would want to live, where in the community he might want to be involved, or even where in this particular community his interests might be able to lead him. He needed a plan and some information about himself to be able to think about these decisions. He also needed more information about the types of opportunities available to him and the places that might allow him to become involved with people who have similar interests.

Michelle

Michelle's needs were more complex; she would need some assistance to live in the community, to find ways to connect with others in a meaningful way, to identify recreation and

101

leisure interests, and to get around in general. However, it wasn't yet clear to Mr. David or to Michelle's transition team whether she wanted to live on her own or make changes in her lifestyle regarding what she currently depended on the support of her family to do. Transition planning, Mr. David knew, is about making sure that the student and his or her family know the options that exist and make their own decisions for a preferred adult life. But he wasn't sure about where to start in regard to this aspect of transition assessment.

ASSESSMENT OF STUDENT ABILITIES, INTERESTS, AND SUPPORT NEEDS

Educators need to develop a starting point for addressing the community involvement necessary for the successful postschool transition of students. An effective assessment plan must be developed in order to gather the information about students needed for creating appropriate goals and experiences. As a first step in this process, teachers should identify what assessment tools are available to examine different aspects of community involvement and research as well as what tools will gather information about students' interests, strengths, and needs as they pertain to community life and potential community experiences. Then teachers can begin collecting important information about their students' current support needs, functioning, and interests as they pertain to community life. Transition assessments need to address such diverse areas as the following:

- *Community living.* Where will this student live and what are his or her skills related to living independently?

- *Community integration.* What are the opportunities for being involved with others in the community, and what are this student's skills related to participating in those activities?

- *Recreation and leisure.* What does this student like to do for fun and relaxation, and what are his or her skills in participating in those activities independently?

- *Transportation and mobility.* What are the options for getting to and from daily and other activities, and what are the student's abilities to use those means of transportation?

- *Finances.* What are the financial resources that this student will need to achieve his or her adult goals, what are the possible sources of this support, and what are this student's skills in managing his or her money and budgeting?

FORMAL ASSESSMENTS

Many of the formal assessments available that address transition assessment broadly include an assessment of these community living areas. See the earlier chapters for more detail about these assessments, which are included at the end of this book. These assessments in particular were helpful for students like Michelle who have had limited experiences being on their own and who have not already identified preferences in the areas of community living. While the results of interest inventories are related to the student's self-awareness and self-knowledge, they do provide a good starting point for further assessments:

- The Brigance Transition Skills Inventory (TSI; Curriculum Associates, 2010) is a transition assessment designed to support teachers of middle and high school students in identifying students' independent living, postsecondary, and employment skills. This assessment also supports teachers in developing data-driven transition plans by the use of an online management system and the Brigance Transition Skills Activities component. The criterion-referenced assessments in the Brigance TSI examine numerous transition-related areas, including community participation, independent living, postsecondary opportunities, and academic skills (Curriculum Associates, 2010).

- The Supports Intensity Scale (Thompson, Bryant, Campbell, Craig, Hughes, Rotholz, et al., 2004) is another formal assessment available that, while not specifically developed as a transition assessment instrument, does provide valuable information that can improve the quality of a transition plan. This assessment supports teachers in identifying the level of meaningful supports students with intellectual disabilities may need in a variety of areas, including community living, lifelong learning, and social activities. This assessment can provide the transition team with reliable information on the support needs of students in 57 life activities as well as specific information on medical and behavioral support needs.

There are several adaptive behavior scales that are also available to support transition planning in the area of community living and community involvement. Assessments such as The Vineland Adaptive Behavior Scales–Second Edition (Vineland II; Sparrow, Cicchetti, & Balla, 2005), The Adaptive Behavior Assessment System–Second Edition (ABAS-II; Harrison & Oakland, 2003), and The Scales of Independent Behavior–Revised (SIB-R; Bruininks, Woodcock, Weatherman, & Hill, 1997) can also support teachers and individualized education program (IEP) teams in developing appropriate goals and plans for students. These scales help to identify the level of student functioning in several daily tasks needed for success in the community and in other transition domains. For example, The Vineland Adaptive Behavior Scale–Second Edition examines, through multiple perspectives, the student's level of functioning in five domains: maladaptive behavior, motor skills, socialization, daily living skills, and communication. The results from this scale can be used by teachers to set goals in the community for students, to identify starting points and plans for community experiences, and to identify specific accommodations that may be needed in order to help students succeed in community situations.

There are numerous additional assessments that are available for teachers to access and use in their planning and individualizing of community experiences. Researching and utilizing what has already been developed provides a starting point for teachers to begin their information gathering on students' skills and abilities in the community.

Interest Inventories

Understanding the interests and goals of the students is another important component in planning community involvement. *Interest inventories* are assessments designed to understand an individual's areas of interest and the level at which he or she might want to pursue particular experiences. Interest inventories can be given directly to students in both formal and informal formats and can focus directly on topics related to the community. For example, teachers may choose to interview students and ask both open and closed questions related to students' particular interests in community experiences. Teachers may also choose to allow students to independently answer a survey on similar topics. Interest inventories can also be given to the student's parents/guardians so as to gain a perspective of what types of activities the parents/guardians observe the student engaging in at home and/or in their community. The informal information gained from the use of interest inventories is essential in understanding what type of activities the student would want to begin to pursue in the community. This information provides a starting point for the exploration of available opportunities in the community that may meet the individual's goals and interests.

Self-determination assessments also can support teachers in planning for community involvement. Assessments such as the ARC Self-Determination Scale (Wehmeyer and Kelchner, 1995), the AIR Self-Determination Scale (Wolman, Campeau, DuBois, Mithaug, & Stolarski, 1994), and Choicemaker (Martin, Huber-Marshall, Maxson, Jerman, Hughes, Miller, & McGill, 2000) are designed to give transition planning teams information about students' skills and abilities in the construct of self-determination. These assessments provide information about the students' abilities and opportunities to set and achieve goals, to solve problems, and to make decisions. See Chapter 3 for additional information about these and other assessments of student self-determination.

INFORMAL AND ALTERNATIVE/PERFORMANCE-BASED ASSESSMENTS

Informal and alternative/performance-based assessments provide valuable information about student involvement and interest in the community. The majority of what students do in the community occurs after school hours; therefore, it is important to find ways to involve the student and his or her family in this component of transition assessment. The transition team needs to have information about what the student does currently in this domain, what options for participation are available in the student's community, and the student's preferences, interests, and strengths, and needs. Table 7.1 provides a comparison between person-centered planning processes and a more traditional clinical approach to team meetings.

Mr. David used the PICTURE method (Holburn et al., 2007) as the framework for person-centered planning for Michelle. He found the method's steps, with its comparison of what an individual does currently as opposed to what he or she would like to be doing, very useful for transition planning. As with all person-centered planning processes, the information collected from the team is shared on large sheets of newsprint using a combination of words and pictures drawn so that everyone can understand the information. Table 7.2 provides an overview of the components of the PICTURE planning process, while Figure 7.1 is an example from Michelle's PICTURE meeting.

It is important to gather not only information about the students and their abilities but also information on the community programs and activities available for students. In order to facilitate a successful transition plan, transition coordinators and teachers need information about the community in which the students will be living as an adult so that

Table 7.1.   Comparison between person-centered planning procedures and clinical team meetings

Clinical meetings	Person-centered planning
Identify deficits, disorders, and problems	Identify capacities, dreams and aspirations
Learn about the person through testing	Learn about the person informally
Decision making is hierarchical and professional	Person, family, and friends decide and have equal status
Specialized treatment or educational team meetings	Group of friends, family, and professionals at meetings
Problems are within the person	Problems are in the environment
Focus of planning is on fixing the person	Focus of planning is on fixing the environment
Focus is on matching individual with existing services	Focus is on building supports around the individual
Goal is to reduce symptoms	Goal is to enhance the quality of life

From Holburn, S., Gordon, A., & Vietze, P.M. (2007). *Person-centered planning made easy: The PICTURE method* (p. 6). Baltimore, MD: Paul H. Brookes Publishing Co.; reprinted by permission.

Table 7.2. PICTURE planning components

Component	Critical questions
Places	Where does this student go now in the community? Where does he or she like or dislike to go?
	Where and how often does he or she go to church, engage in fun/recreation, in social interaction, or dine out?
	How often does he or she visit a grocery store, shopping mall, hairstylist, bank, or restaurant?
	How does this individual get to these places? Who goes with him or her?
	Does he or she have money to spend?
	Does he or she visit friends and/or family in the community?
	How can he or she have greater opportunities to experience new places and visit more places that are preferred?
Competence	What skills does this individual have that enable inclusion?
	What skills cold be developed to enhance inclusion as an adult? What supports are in place to help this person be included in his or her community?
	What supports would be necessary to help this individual meet his or her goals for the future?
Respect	What roles does this individual assume now? What is the nature of these roles?
	What valued community roles could be developed?
Physical/behavioral health	What is this person's current health concerns/issues?
	What does he or she know about maintaining health, such as eating well, taking medication, seeking medical/dental care, and following recommendations of health care providers?
	Can he or she exercise, and in what kinds of exercise does he or she participate?
	Are there behavioral concerns? Can he or she use self-management strategies?
Choices	What choices does this student make now?
	What choices would he or she like to make?
	What could be done to support/facilitate choices for his or her?
Work or daytime activities	Who are the people with whom this individual interacts during the day?
	Who are the supportive individuals?
	Who are the people who could be involved in making work a more supportive environment?
Relationships	What are the current relationships that this individual has?
	What relationships could be developed/improved?
	With whom does this person live?
	With whom does he or she work, participate in activities, and/or go to school?
	Who are the members of his or her family?
	With whom in the community does he or she have contact?
	Who are this person's friends?
	Who helps him or her?
	Are there relationships that should be strengthened?
	Are there relationships that will be ending?
Home	Where and with whom does this individual live now?
	Where does this individual want to live after high school?
	What does he or she do at home in terms of cooking, cleaning, general maintenance, paying bills, or other general household activities?
	Does he or she plan to live with someone else?
Next steps	What can we do to facilitate this student's transition to greater community inclusion?

From Holburn, S., Gordon, A., & Vietze, P.M. (2007). *Person-centered planning made easy: The PICTURE method* (pp. 26, 28–31). Baltimore, MD: Paul H. Brookes Publishing Co.; adapted by permission.

they are able to help the students understand the big picture of the supports they would need in order to attain his or her vision for adult life. Community resource mapping is one strategy that can help with collecting this information about the services available in a specific community as well as opportunities for community jobs, living, recreation and leisure, and involvement.

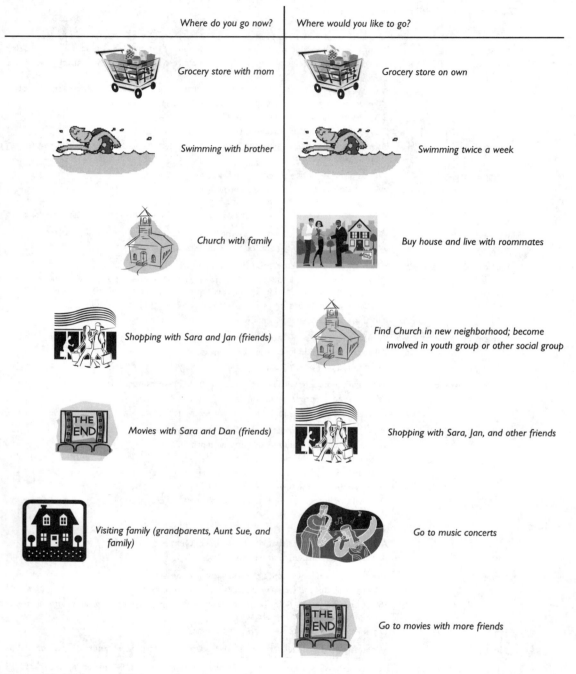

Figure 7.1. Michelle's Places Map: Where she goes or wants to go. (*Source:* Sonoran University Center for Excellence in Developmental Disabilities, 2011.)

Community Resource Mapping

Community resource mapping is a graphic representation of the various services, organizations, supports, and opportunities within a community (Crane & Mooney, 2005). The goal of community resource mapping is to ensure that students have access to an integrated and comprehensive system of services in the community by conducting a systematic inventory of what already exists. There are four steps involved in conducting this community assessment of services: "pre-mapping, mapping, taking action, and Maintaining, Sustaining, and Evaluating Mapping Efforts" (National Center on Secondary Education and Transition, 2005, p. 2). Each of these phases engages the teacher and the other team members to strategically plan, with an accurate picture of available opportunities, for how to engage in the community as well to identify and connect with the individuals, agencies, and businesses that are linked to those opportunities. Getzel, Deschamps, and Thoma point out that community resource mapping can provide information about specifics of a community "such as the reliability of transportation, available jobs, resources for health care, and accessibility of retail and grocery stores" (2010, p. 180).

Mr. David knew that neither he nor the teachers who worked directly with students with disabilities could conduct community resource maps for every student and do so in a manner that would be sufficiently detailed enough to support a successful, comprehensive transition plan. However, by involving other team members in this part of the assessment process, he could be certain that this information would be part of their planning process. Chris could complete a community resource map with a group of his friends, while Michelle could do it with the support of her older brother and/or a parent. Students can take pictures of the various buildings in the neighborhood and add them to a map so as to develop a graphic representation of the community. A separate form can provide more detailed information about the kinds of places, supports, and services that exist in the community. The Community Mapping Results form (see Figure 7.2) is an example of a form that Mr. David provided to Chris and Michelle to use in order to document the information they collected.

COLLECTING SPECIFIC ASSESSMENT DATA IN THE COMMUNITY

After learning information about students' functioning and interests and identifying community resources and partners, teachers and/or transition coordinators can begin to think about various ways in which students can participate in their community more successfully in these settings. Teachers must consider how to assess the demands of potential community experiences in order to develop appropriate plans for students. One must understand how to assess environmental demands and student growth in meeting these demands.

Ecological Inventory

To develop both the proper supports and the correct community experiences for students, teachers must also assess the environment in which students are actively participating. Ecological inventories serve as one type of environmental assessment that focuses on identifying the specific demands of a particular setting. Conducting an ecological inventory of an environment is one way to assess its physical and situational demands. Ecological inventories require teachers and/or service providers to systematically assess both the overall environments and the smaller settings or subenvironments where students might spend a lot of their time. For example, if a student is volunteering as a swim instructor at the local YMCA, the ecological inventory will first consider the overall environment of the YMCA (i.e., reception area, exercise equipment room, classrooms, preschool room, and pool area) and record information such as lighting, physical environment, safety issues, spacing of equipment and furniture, required social interactions, and the overall crowds. However, teachers need to look more closely at the specific setting in which the

Community Mapping Results

Restaurants		Sports and games	
a. Fast food		a. Participant	
b. Ethnic restaurants		b. Observer	
c. Eclectic food		Exercise/fitness	
d. Bars, grills		Theaters	
Computer training classes		Arts and crafts instruction or supplies	
Gas/auto maintenance		Transportation	
		Groceries	
Tax assistance		Hair cutting, styling	
Clothing stores		Clinics, emergency care	
Home furnishings		Veterinary clinics	
		Dental care	
Child care		Home maintenance	
Bookstores		Car washes	
CDs/DVDs		Convenience stores	
Public parks		Other places	

Figure 7.2 Community mapping results.

From Thoma, C.A., & Wehman, P. (2010). *Getting the most out of IEPs: An educator's guide to the student-directed approach* (p. 182). Baltimore, MD: Paul H. Brookes Publishing Co.; reprinted by permission. In *Demystifying Transition Assessment* by Colleen A. Thoma, Ph.D., and Ronald Tamura, Ph.D. (2013 by Paul H. Brookes Publishing Co., Inc.)

student is working (the pool area) and collect additional information such as noise level, communication requirements, square footage, amount of people working and accessing the environment, specific tasks that need to be carried out, and the routines and rules within the setting.

Assessing the environment and taking detailed notes on its physical demands will help support teachers as they develop proper support plans for students entering into the community. Teachers can assess the specific tasks that students must engage in while participating in that environment and develop task analyses to support students in completing them. For example, if the student is responsible for greeting individuals and having them sign in for their group swim lessons, teachers must assess which specific skills are needed to accomplish this. Conducting an assessment of both the task demands and the environment in which the tasks must be carried out can assist the teacher in creating an effective task analysis plan that is tailored specifically to that particular environment. Further, teachers can gain a clear picture of how students are able to carry out the tasks in that environment and can take data on how they are progressing toward their goals in that community setting. Figure 7.3 is an example of a data sheet that Mr. David used to conduct an ecological inventory of the YMCA, for Chris, and the grocery store, for Michelle.

Situational Assessments

Once the specific demands of the environment have been identified, an assessment of the student's ability to succeed within those demands can be assessed. Direct observation of the student's functioning in that environment is imperative in the transition planning process. By directly observing the student engaged in the community experience, teachers can determine additional supports the student may need. Task analyses can be generated to help a student accomplish specific tasks within the community experience and can help teachers assess how the student is progressing toward set goals. Further, teachers can look at numerous factors related to student success in the environment. For example, is the student engaged? Is he or she completing tasks in an efficient amount of time? Is he or she communicating with others around him or her? Is he or she happy in the environment? Does he or she need prompting to meet any of the environmental or task demands? Direct observations can provide a comprehensive picture of the student's attitudes and abilities in that particular situation or setting. Teachers can formulate individualized progress monitoring checklists for students to collect data on his or her progress and can chart his or her growth over time. The accuracy of this data, however, is dependent on having a full understanding of the environmental demands and having clear objectives on what the student should accomplish within that environment. Figure 7.4 is an example of a task analysis used to conduct a situational assessment of Michelle's use of an ATM machine to withdraw cash.

SUMMARY

There are a number of strategies that are helpful in conducting an assessment of student strengths, needs, preferences, and interests in the community integration/inclusion domains of community living, recreation and leisure, community involvement, and transportation/mobility. Of course, these are very different skills and tasks, but the overall approach to assessment can be the same in each of these areas. First, teachers need a way to identify student goals for the future in these areas. Second, teachers needs to identify

Ecological Inventory

Location: _____ Address: _____
Time of observation: _____ Distance from school/home: _____

1. Draw a picture of the physical layout of the setting.

2. What, if any, unusual characteristics are present in the setting?

3. Is the physical environment accessible for the student? If not, what would it take to make the setting physically accessible?

4. What are the subenvironments in this setting? For each potential subenvironment, identify the activities that occur in which this individual would need to participate.

Subenvironment: _____ Subenvironment: _____
Activities: _____ Activities: _____
_____ _____
_____ _____
_____ _____

Were employees nearby? ____Yes ____No   Were employees nearby? _____Yes _____No
Subenvironment: _____ Subenvironment: _____

Activities: _____ Activities: _____
_____ _____
_____ _____

Were employees nearby? ____Yes ____No   Were employees nearby? _____Yes _____No

5. What is the climate of the setting? For example, are staff friendly? How do employees treat customers?

6. Are there safety concerns for participating in this setting?

7. How does this setting match the preferences of the individual?

8. What IEP/transition goals could be addressed by participating in this setting?

9. Are there specific requirements of participating in this setting that this individual cannot meet?

Figure 7.3. Ecological inventory.

Adapted from *Ecological Inventory* Form by Dymond, S. in *Functional Curriculum for Elementary and Secondary Students with Special Needs, Third Edition* (p. 383–384), by J. Kregel & P. Wehman (Eds.), 2012, Austin, TX: PRO-ED. Copyright 2012 by PRO-ED, Inc. Adapted with permission. In *Demystifying Transition Assessment* by Colleen A. Thoma, Ph.D., and Ronald Tamura, Ph.D. (2013, Paul H. Brookes Publishing Co., Inc.)

Step	Performs independently		Performs with verbal prompting		Performs with visual prompts		Does not perform	
	Consistently	Occasionally	Consistently	Occasionally	Consistently	Occasionally	Consistently	Occasionally
Approaches ATM								
Removes ATM card from wallet								
Inserts card into machine, magnetic strip down and to left								
Selects language to be used								
Enters PIN number								
Selects type of transaction								
Selects specific account to be used for transaction								
Enters amount of transaction								
Verifies amount requested								
Selects Yes or No when asked whether receipt is requested								
Remains at ATM while request is processed								
Collects money when dispensed								
Puts money in wallet								
Selects transaction complete when prompted								
Takes receipt when dispensed								
Takes card when dispensed								
Places receipt and card in wallet								
Leaves ATM area								

Figure 7.4. Task analysis of the use of an ATM. (*Source:* Kregel, 2012.)

the student's current activities, supports, and skills and the available opportunities in the student's own community. Then specific information can be collected about the skill requirements and available supports in those environments and the student's individual ability to meet those requirements. That information, considered collectively, can serve to identify annual transition IEP goals that can help support a successful transition to an adult life in the community.

8

Making Sense of Transition Assessment Data

Colleen A. Thoma and Ronald Tamura

Now that you have been introduced to and, hopefully, administered assessments in the areas of academics, self-determination, employment, postsecondary education, health, and community, there is still another step in the transition assessment process. You still need to make sense of the data and use it to help students achieve their goals for their adult lives. But how do you organize the data you have collected so that it can be useful to the transition individualized education program (IEP) team members for this important task? This chapter will provide guidance in helping you use this data to identify the following:

1. The vision for a student's future

2. The requirements of environments into which the student will be transitioning

3. The annual goals that will help the student move toward his or her vision for adult life

4. The transition services that a student might need in order to be successful in postschool settings or to transition to postschool settings

5. The overall progress the student has made in achieving both annual goals and his or her long-term goals for adult life

VISION FOR THE FUTURE

As stated in Chapter 1, the first step in using a backward planning process is articulating a clear picture of each student's vision for adult life. Data from multiple assessments can be used to "develop" this picture of the future for students, with some of the most helpful being those that provide an opportunity for the student to describe his or her vision across multiple transition domains. Person-centered planning processes and/or assessments that are part of self-determined transition curricula are useful tools for this process. Person-centered planning processes such as Making Action PlanS (MAPS; Forest & Pearpoint, 1992), Planning Alternative Tomorrows with Hope (PATH) plans (Pearpoint, O'Brien, & Forest, 1993), and Personal Futures Planning (Mount, 2000) among others give students and families a chance to discuss their visions while seeking input from a number of partners. Not only can school personnel be part of this process, but so can extended family, neighbors, friends, or others who bring information to the planning process that others lack or do not have in sufficient depth to inform the planning process. This component of transition planning is referred to as seeking multiple resources and perspectives (Thoma, Bartholomew, & Scott, 2009) and is particularly important when a student's vision for the future includes elements that are unfamiliar to the other members of the transition team or when additional creative individuals are needed to identify necessary supports and/or services that could help make a vision real. See below for an example.

While person-centered planning procedures provide an opportunity to bring in multiple resources and perspectives, using assessments that are part of self-determination transition curricula such as *Whose Future Is It Anyway?* (Wehmeyer, Lawrence, Kelchner, Palmer, Garner, & Soukup, 2004), *Next S.T.E.P.* (Halpern, Herr, Wolf, Doren, Johnson, & Lawson, 2000) and *Choicemaker* (Martin, Marshall, & DePry, 2008) can provide more detailed information about a vision for the future as well as information about student skills in making those dreams a reality. Most of them provide an assessment component that the student and one or two others complete, providing information about student performance in multiple settings. This information is then used to develop a more complete profile of the student's preferences, interests, strengths, and needs.

A summary of the information collected through a person-centered planning process and/or a self-determined transition assessment process can be communicated to the other members of the transition IEP team using a number of different methods. Some students might want to communicate this information verbally, but most will want a type of graphic representation of this information. While Michelle's information was summarized on a one-page form (see Figure 3.4 for this example), Chris chose to develop a PowerPoint presentation to highlight his goals for the future and use it to share with his transition IEP team. He used an IEP template, which is a component of many student-led IEP processes (Thoma & Wehman, 2010). There are a number of web sites that provide information about conducting student-led IEP meetings, including templates for developing a PowerPoint slide that students can use. Table 8.1 provides a list of some of those online resources.

Person-Centered Planning

Mr. David knew very little about the world of fashion, but he still needed to coordinate the transition plan for a student, Takisha, who liked reading through fashion magazines, was good at helping others find the perfect accessory to pull together an outfit, and thought that she might want to be a fashion designer. It was Mr. David's job to help identify job experiences for students and to coordinate their on-the-job training, but he was at a loss when it came to knowing how to do that for Takisha. When he and Takisha worked together to send out invitations to her person-centered planning meeting, they agreed that it would be a good idea to include two individuals who could provide information about the world of fashion design. First, they invited Ms. Sheryl, the high school educator who teaches courses in sewing, fashion, and interior design. They also invited Mr. Roberts, an instructor of fashion design at a local university, who had a number of connections with professionals in the field. These two individuals were able to describe multiple careers/jobs in the fashion industry and corresponding educational and experiential requirements, and they provided contacts for Mr. David and Takisha to use for job shadowing and/or internship opportunities. Ultimately, Takisha's entry into the fashion design world as an assistant was facilitated by having these two people added to her team.

Table 8.1.   Resources for involving students in the IEP process

Resource	Contact information	IEP stage	Suggested grades	Materials included
Can I go to the IEP meeting?	http://www.ldonline.org/article/6304	Planning	None suggested	Questions students should ask themselves to learn more about their strengths
Student-led IEP Template	http://www.vermiliontpc.com/iep/student-led_iep_001.htm	Drafting, meeting	High school/transition-aged students	PowerPoint template for student-led transition IEP meeting
Helping students develop their IEPs: Student guide and Technical assistance guide	http://nichcy.org/wp-content/uploads/docs/st1.pdf http://nichcy.org/wp content/uploads/docs/ta2.pdf	Drafting	Older students	Student guide (for learning about IEP and how to prepare for meeting) Technical assistance guide (for suggestions on teaching students about their IEPs)
Student involvement in IEPs templates	The "I'm Determined" web site http://www.imdetermined.org/student_involvement	Planning, drafting, meeting	All ages: Preschool–secondary	PowerPoint template and other materials and resources to help students prepare for their IEP meetings (knowing their rights and responsibilities), plan postsecondary goals and IEP content, and be actively involved in the IEP meeting
IEP portfolio template	http://hawbaker.pls.iowapages.org/id2.html	Drafting, meeting	None suggested	Article on planning and implementation strategies that includes lessons, an implementation action plan, sample IEP portfolio pages, and student perspectives IEP portfolio template for student use as a guide to lead an IEP meeting
How to help students lead their IEP meetings	See Mason, McGahee-Kovac, & Johnson (2004)	Meeting	None suggested	Teacher's guide to instruct students on how to participate in or lead their IEP meetings
Developing student competence in self-directed IEPs	See Torgerson, Miner, & Shen (2004)	Meeting	Secondary	Teacher's guide to train students to be involved in their IEP meetings
Checklist for student-led IEP	See Figure 3.1 (Martin, Marshall, Maxson, & Jerman, 1996)	Drafting, meeting	Secondary	Sample checklist for IEP presentation during a student-led IEP team meeting

From Uphold, N.M., Walker, A.R., & West, D.W. (2007). Resources for involving students in their IEP process. *TEACHING Exceptional Children Plus, 3*(4), Article 1. © 2007 by the authors, licensed to the public under the Creative Commons Attribution License.

For Michelle, like most students with significant disabilities who struggle with communication, the information collected from person-centered planning processes and the self-determination curriculum provided only a starting point, which was then used to identify additional assessments that could help her become more specific about her preferences and interests. Her transition assessment process also included a number of performance-based assessment activities that provided experiences she could use to help her make decisions. This information could be used by members of her transition team to ask more specific questions about her plans for the future instead of the open-ended questions like "What kind of job do you want to have?" Michelle's answer to that question was that she didn't know. However, when the questions became more specific and designed to help her reflect back on experiences she'd had, her answers could be more concrete and provide guidance to identify next steps. For example, Mr. David could ask questions like "You had a chance to work in a hospital's supply room—what did you like about it, and what didn't you like about it?" When Michelle said that she did not want to have a job in a hospital, she was able to indicate that it was the lack of interaction with others that was the main reason that she was dissatisfied with the job. Mr. David could use that information to find another job option in a hospital setting where there was more interaction with others as well as other jobs in other settings that also had more interaction with others. The answers to these specific questions provide guidance for identifying subsequent work experiences that build on student preferences while minimizing those things they do not prefer.

Mr. David sat down with Michelle, her parents, and her teacher to summarize the information they had collected about Michelle's vision for adult life from all of these various assessments. He used the columns shown in Table 8.2 to organize the information they currently had about Michelle's vision for adult life, which helped them identify situational, performance-based assessment information that they still needed to collect.

Once those additional assessment procedures were identified for Michelle, Mr. David found it helpful to summarize information collected from the various transition assessments and information gathered from the situational and performance-based assessments. The information about a student's vision for his or her adult life and the specific information that was collected from these procedures for Chris are found in Figure 8.1.

REQUIREMENTS OF POSTSCHOOL ENVIRONMENTS

Once a clear vision for a student's postschool, adult life has been identified, the next step is using the transition assessment data to determine the specific supports a student will need in order to be successful in those settings. While in the past, educators might have used this information to determine whether there was a "match" between the requirements of a specific environment and a student's existing skills, this is too simplistic of an approach for a number of reasons. First and most importantly, even if a student does not currently possess the skills needed so as to be successful in a specific environment, it does not necessarily mean that he or she could not *learn* those skills if taught. Second, a number of accommodations, supports, or modifications could be used to bridge the

Table 8.2.   Postschool planning tool

What do you want to do when you leave high school?

Expressed	Tested	Observed
Student, parents, and other transition team members	*Age-appropriate transition assessment*	*School/work experiences*
Michelle has not indicated an expressed preference	*Alternative Assessments based on Academic Achievement Standards (AA-AAS)— checklists, observations, performance assessments, student work and portfolios*	Community observation
		Job analysis
Parents would like her to be happy, have some work, have friends, and enjoy a variety of recreation and leisure activities		Situational assessments
	Reading Free Vocational Interest Inventory (RFVII-2)	*Syracuse Community-Referenced Curriculum Guide**
Team agrees with parents' vision and would like Michelle to work, enjoy a variety of recreation and leisure activities, and be more self-reliant	*ARC (Self-Determination Scale)*	*Vineland Behavior Scale—Second Edition**
	AIR (Self-Determination)	*Behavior Assessment System for Children (BASC-2)**
	Enderle-Severson Transition Rating Scales— 3rd Edition (ESTRS 3rd Ed.)	
	Positive Personal Profile (PPP)	
	Your Child's Health Care Independence Worksheet 2 for Parents of Youth Age 15–17	

*Falls under the categorization of an age-appropriate transition assessment and is observed

Student: __Chris_____   IEP date: _____06/12/12_____

Academic Assessments

Academic content	Grade-level performance	Standardized test performance	Accommodations/ modifications
Reading	Chris's score: 20 Benchmark: 21	ACT	None needed
Math	Chris's score: 27 Benchmark: 22	ACT	None needed
English	Chris's score: 18 Benchmark: 18	ACT	None needed
Science	Chris's score: 25 Benchmark: 24	ACT	None needed
Writing	Chris's score: 5 Benchmark: 7	ACT	None needed
Progress toward school requirements	All credits earned and on track for graduation	High school graduation testing requirements	None needed

Other Assessments Required by IDEA 2004

Area	Current performance	Prior assessment	Current accommodations	Assessments needed
Behavior	N/A	N/A	N/A	N/A
Assistive technology	None	None	None	Assistive technology support checklist
Time with peers who don't have disabilities	100% of the day	None	Organization support, writing and reading support	
Participation in standardized assessments	Yes	Every other year for standardized assessment	None	ACT, high school graduation standardized testing
Communication	Age appropriate			
Braille	N/A	N/A	N/A	N/A

Self-Determination/Transition Assessments

Area	Current level	Preferences	Summary of assessments	Assessments needed
Knowledge of self and disability	Scored 93 on AIR		AIR Self-Determination Scale	None
Transition: employment	Not interested in working	Would like to work— maybe part-time in college/university	Will be taking ASVAB, CAPS, and O*NET	ASVAB CAPS O*NET
Transition: postsecondary education	Scored below benchmark in reading and writing on ACT	Wants to go to college/university	Has taken ACT	Transition Assessment and Goal Generator (TAGG)
Transition: functional skills	Age appropriate			
Transition: independent living	Difficulty understanding health care needs and role with doctor during appointments		Health & Wellness 101: Basic Skills CASEY	
Transition: adult services	Needs to establish connections			

Figure 8.1. Individual education program (IEP) assessment planning form. (*Source:* Thoma & Wehman, 2010.)

gap between a student's current skills and the requirements of the environment (O'Brien & Callahan, 2010). Third, the mismatch might not be as significant as indicated by the assessment (Thoma, Boyd, & Austin, 2012). Educators need to verify their perception that a specific skill is absolutely essential for success in a specific setting; sometimes tasks can be eliminated or picked up by others with little negative impact on the goals of the setting. This technique has been used by job coaches for years through a process called job carving (Wehman & Brooke, 2012). These approaches should be thoroughly explored before determining that a specific environment would not work for a student. At that point, changes to the environment-student mismatch could also be explored. Such changes could include the following:

- Looking at a similar outcome but in a different setting (such as the same job but with a different employer)

- Exploring changes that could be made in the same setting (such as through job carving)

- Determining whether a change is necessary in the expectation of the transition team (such as when an employer perceives a skill as being less critical than the assessor does)

A decision-making process to make sense of the assessment of the requirements of a specific environment and a student's ability to meet those requirements is provided in Figure 8.2, and information that helps with identifying why a student is not performing a skill and what to do about it is included in Table 8.3.

HOW TO USE THE ASSESSMENT DATA TO SET GOALS

The third use of transition assessment data is to identify the annual transition IEP goals that are necessary to help students meet their postschool goals for an adult life. As described throughout this book, educators collect transition assessment data across the range of transition domains, which includes the following:

1. Academic skills

2. Self-determination

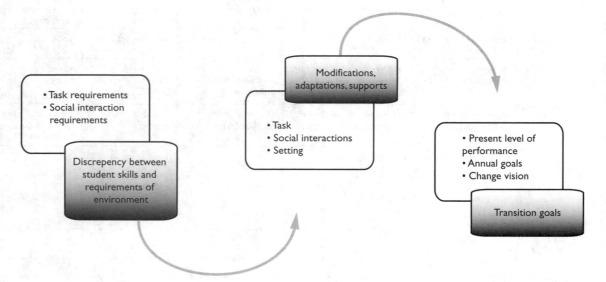

Figure 8.2. Requirements of postschool environments.

Table 8.3. Making the "Can't," "Doesn't," or "Won't" determination

Observed student behavior	Instructional conclusion	Intervention
Can't		
The student has not been observed performing the skill(s) in current or recent settings.	The student does not have behavior in repertoire.	Teach the skill in stages.
Doesn't		
The student has demonstrated that he or she knows the skill, but he or she does not use it consistently.	The student is not sure when to use the skill; positive reinforcement is not strong enough (or payoff for a competing behavior is stronger).	Find a more effective replacement behavior and reinforce it consistently; teach student when to use the skill.
Won't		
The student has demonstrated (or verbalized) that he or she knows how and under what circumstances to use the skill but either refuses to use it consistently or uses it in an inappropriate or exaggerated way.	The skill is in the student's repertoire, but he or she lacks the self-confidence, self-control, or decision-making skills to perform it appropriately.	Determine the reason for nonperformance. Teach self-control, teach replacement behaviors, or recommend further study by an interdisciplinary team.

Adapted from *Social Skills* by Pankaskie, S. & Chandler, S. in *Functional Curriculum for Elementary and Secondary Students with Special Needs, Third Edition* (p. 294), by J. Kregel & P. Wehman (Eds.), 2012, Austin, TX: PRO-ED. Copyright 2012 by PRO-ED, Inc. Adapted with permission.

3. Employment

4. Postsecondary education

5. Health

6. Community

Besides information about specific transition assessment information, a student and his or her transition team also need to consider a student's current performance in school and, in particular, in academic classes as they develop an educational program for the coming year. This current performance is summarized in a component of the IEP document known as the *Present level of performance* or *PLOP*. The PLOP must include information about a student's academic performance as well as functional performance. To be sure that all relevant information was included in writing the present level of performance and, ultimately, in writing the annual transition IEP goals, educators can use a form similar to the one found in Figure 1.4 to record all the relevant data. Keeping an electronic version of this transition assessment checklist provides an opportunity for educators and students, if appropriate, to update the information collected throughout the year so that all relevant information is considered when this information is shared with the team at the next IEP meeting.

Once all the recorded data are summarized in a manageable way, educators then can use that information to set appropriate goals for students. These transition goals have to be 1) measurable, 2) specific to a setting, 3) observable, and 4) related to the postschool goals of the specific student. The goals also need to be aligned with the requirements of IDEA 2004, which require that the IEP for students who are at the ages of 16 years or older must include "Appropriate measurable postsecondary goals based on *age-appropriate transition assessments* related to training, education, employment, and, where appropriate, independent living skills" (34 C.F.R. 300.320 [b] and [c] 20 U.S.C. 1414 [d][1][A][i][VIII]).

A student and his or her transition team use multiple sources of information to identify the annual transition goals. The Secondary Transition Planning Process form (see Figure 8.3) provides a form that educators can use to summarize a student's assessment data and PLOP and then, depending on the assessment information collected, identify whether an instructional goal, a modification/accommodation, or a new goal is required.

TRANSITION SERVICES AND INTERAGENCY LINKAGES

The fourth use of transition assessment data is to identify transition services and interagency linkages that would be needed by a student to achieve his or her goals for adult life. To be sure he was identifying the necessary supports the student would need, Mr. David knew that he needed to know both the vision for a student's adult life and the information, gathered from an ecological inventory of those postschool settings, about whether a student had the skills to be successful. He wouldn't know whether Michelle needed the support of a job coach in order to be successful at work until he identified the job she wanted to do, the supports that already existed there, and any discrepancy between the demands of the environment and Michelle's current abilities. The same was true of Chris's needs. He wanted to go to college after high school, but the type of college and the type of undergraduate program in which he would enroll would require different types of supports in order for him to be successful. Mr. David found that performance-based assessment information was particularly useful in meeting this goal of transition planning and helped the transition planning team be more creative in identifying necessary linkages (which might include services and supports that go beyond those provided exclusively to individuals with disabilities). For instance, Michelle wanted to live in her own apartment after high school, but financially, doing so was beyond her income level. The transition team identified that resources for housing available to those with low income (Section 8 housing) as well as a roommate referral service both were necessary interagency linkages available to help her meet this transition goal. The Organizing Student Direction of Adult Supports form (see Figure 8.4) provides a way to identify necessary links to adult service agencies that can help students achieve their goals for adult life as well as organize the steps necessary to contact those agencies (i.e., contact information, who will make the contact, and what information will be necessary).

MEASURING PROGRESS

The fifth use of transition assessment data is to monitor progress or lack of progress toward meeting annual and long-range transition goals. This part of the transition assessment process is just as important as the other four uses for data, since students with disabilities will learn more about their preferences and interests as they begin to work on these goals, have new experiences, and have this chance to learn more about themselves. So as Mr. David began to investigate tools and strategies he could use to monitor student progress toward meeting goals, he looked specifically for ways that he could involve students in this process. This was another way that Mr. David felt he could increase student self-determination in the transition planning process.

Mr. David used a simple goal planning template available in Microsoft Word to provide a way that he could involve students in the process of self-monitoring their progress toward meeting their transition goals. The Student Goal Sheet form (see Figure 8.5) is the goal setting template that he found to be useful for students with a range of support needs: Students like Chris can record their own information and data using this form as it is. Michelle could use some adaptations to the form to add pictures or to include summary information from a teacher and/or paraprofessional—and she could even have others add information to the

Secondary Transition Planning Process

What do you want to do when you leave high school?

Expressed	Tested	Observed
Student states (parents)	*Age-appropriate transition assessment*	*School work/work experiences*

Age-Appropriate Transition Assessment

List of assessment(s):_____ Date(s):_____

Needs	Strengths	Preferences	Interests
Additional Information found from the assessment(s)			

Present Level

Current level of performance	Strengths	Concerns	Impact statement

Postschool Outcome Goal Statements/Goals/Objectives

Employment:
Goal:
Objective:
Objective:
Objective:

Figure 8.3. Secondary transition planning process.

Demystifying Transition Assessment by Colleen A. Thoma, Ph.D., and Ronald Tamura, Ph.D.

(continued)

Postsecondary education/training:
Goal:
Objective:
Objective:
Objective:

If applicable, independent living skills:
Goal:
Objective:
Objective:
Objective:

Coordinated Set of Activities

	Employment	Post-secondary ed/training	Independent living skills
Course of study			
Transition services			
Related services			

Organizing Student Direction of Adult Supporters

Transition planning area	What do I want to do?	What supports am I getting now?	What supports will I need in the future?	Who could provide these?	How do I contact them?	What will I need to get their help?
Work						
Home						
Learning						
Health						
Friends						
Fun						
Getting around						
Money						

Figure 8.4. Organizing student direction of adult supporters.

From Thoma, C.A., & Wehman, P. (2010). *Getting the most out of IEPs: An educator's guide to the student-directed approach* (p. 179). Baltimore, MD: Paul H. Brookes Publishing Co.; reprinted by permission. In *Demystifying Transition Assessment* by Colleen A. Thoma, Ph.D., and Ronald Tamura, Ph.D. (2013 by Paul H. Brookes Publishing Co., Inc.)

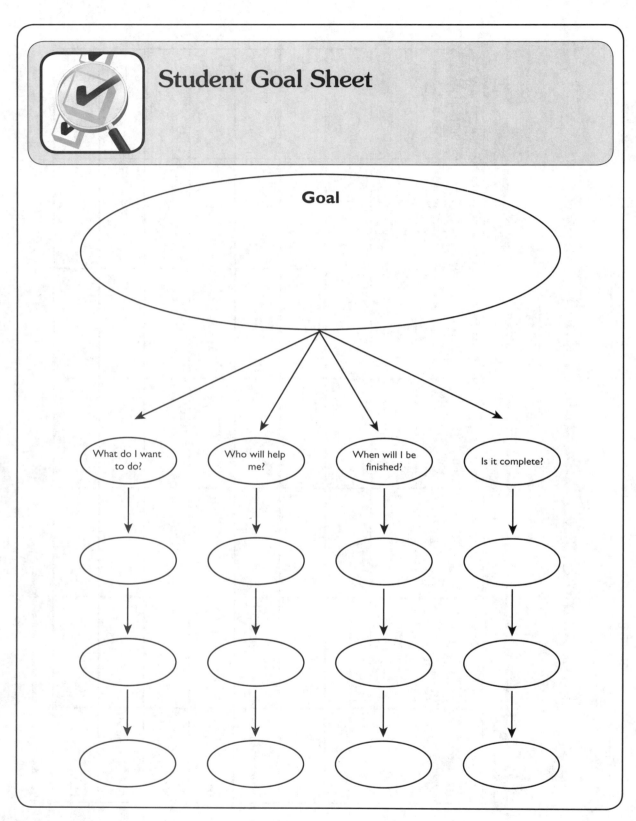

Figure 8.5. Student goal sheet.

Student Goal Sheet

Transition Area	Key	Goals and Objectives		
Education and training	4	I will take a geography class.	Start	Finish
	4-A	Look through the schedule of classes to see what is available.		
	4-B	Talk to the geography teacher about what I need to pass this class.		
	4-C	Write down what I will do in this class, how I will do it, and who will help me.		
Jobs	5	I will begin to explore jobs that match my interests and what I do well.		
	5-A	I will go to the library and read some books or articles about jobs.		
	5-B	I will complete two different career surveys.		
	5-C	I will meet with the job coordinator and find out what jobs may be open to me.		
Living on my own	6	I will learn skills I need to live on my own.		
	6-A	I will open a savings account.		
	6-B	I will manage my own pocket money by writing down what I spend each day.		
	6-C	I will use the telephone to get and give information.		

Figure 8.6. Goals and objectives. (Adapted by permission from Held, M.F., Thoma, C.A., & Thomas, K. [2004]. "The John Jones Show": How one teacher facilitated transition planning for a young man with autism. *Focus on Autism and Other Developmental Disabilities, 19*(3), 177–188. Reprinted from Held, M.F., & Thoma, C.A. [2003, December]. *Facilitating self-determination; What happens after the meeting.* Presented at the TASH Conference, Chicago, IL.)

form that she could bring back to Mr. David, who could then help her use the data to make decisions about what happens next. This form could be used to collect information about a specific transition IEP goal, subsequent transition assessment data, and/or a combination of transition goals.

Mr. David knew how important it was to not only monitor progress on transition IEP goals himself, with the assistance of the student, but also to communicate progress with other transition IEP team members. For any IEP goal, it is necessary to communicate progress with a student's parents or guardians at least as often as report cards go home to parents of all students. However, with transition planning and services, there are a number of stakeholders who need updates about student progress that would be more frequent than annual meetings. For this purpose, Mr. David found that providing a listing of a student's current IEP goals with target dates and space to indicate current progress worked well for this level of ongoing communication with transition team members. Of course, this required student and/or parent approval to share this information with transition team members, but for those who wanted this level of communication, Mr. David found that this format helped facilitate the process. See Figure 8.6 for an example of this communication tool.

CONCLUSION

The efforts of educators to identify and collect student information using multiple transition assessment procedures and instruments are an essential part of a comprehensive, age-appropriate transition assessment process. By collecting data through the use of multiple transition assessment procedures, the information gathered can provide sufficient guidance for the student's self-direction of his or her own transition to adult life. Mr. David found that his efforts to work with teachers to identify what they already were doing, combined with his target transition assessment processes, which supplemented this information rather than duplicated it was a critically important part of the process. He also found that his efforts improved over time as he, the student, and other members of a student's transition team learned more about the student's long-term goals and the skills related to those goals. He and the student stressed less about having *the answer* in the first year of the transition assessment and planning process and realized, instead, that what they learned each year brought them closer to articulating a clear vision for the student's adult life and the supports he or she needed in order to make that life a reality.

References

ACT. (2007). *ACT test*. Iowa City, IA: Author.

ACT. (2010). *A first look at the common core and college and career readiness*. Iowa City, IA: Author. Retrieved from http://www.act.org/commoncore

Action For Healthy Kids (2011) Annual Report. Retrieved on March 12, 2012. From, http://www.actionforhealthy kids.org/media-center/annual-reports/action-for-healthy -kids-2011.pdf

AHEAD. (2004). *Best practices resources*. Huntersville, NC: Association on Higher Education and Disability. Retrieved from http://www.ahead.org/resources/best-practices -resources

Ainsworth, L. (2003). *Unwrapping the standards: A simple process to make standards manageable*. Englewood, CO: Lead + Learn Press.

American College of Obstetricians and Gynecologists. (2011). Alcohol, tobacco and other substance use and abuse. In *Guidelines for adolescent health care* (2nd ed., pp. 97–110). Washington, DC: Author.

Artiles, A.J., Trent, S.C., & Palmer, J. (2004). Culturally diverse students in special education: Legacies and prospects. In J.A. Banks & C.M. Banks (Eds.), *Handbook of research on multicultural education* (2nd ed., pp. 716–735). San Francisco, CA: Jossey-Bass.

Banerjee, M. (2010). Technology trends for students with disabilities. In S.F. Shaw, J.W. Madaus, & L.L. Dukes III (Eds.), *Preparing students with disabilities for college success: A practical guide to transition planning*. Baltimore, MD: Paul H. Brookes Publishing Co.

Becker, R. (2000). *Reading-free vocational interest inventory: 2 (R-FVII:2)* (2nd ed.). Retrieved from http://transi-tioncoalition.org/transition/assessment_review/view .php?id=36

Bennett, G.K. (2006). *Bennett mechanical comprehension test*, 2nd ed. San Antonio, TX: Pearson.

Benz, M., Lindstrom, L., & Yovanoff, P. (2000). Improving graduation and employment outcomes of students with disabilities: Predictive factors and student perspectives. *Exceptional Children, 66*, 509–529.

Bergin, C.A., & Bergin, D.A. (2010). Sleep: The E-ZZZ intervention. *Educational Leadership, 67*(4), 44–47.

Black, R.S., & Ornellas, C. (2001). Assessment of social competence and social networks for transition. *Assessment for Effective Intervention, 26*(4), 23–39.

Blum, R., Garell, D., & Hodgman C. (1993). Transition from child-centered to adult health-care systems for adolescents with chronic conditions: A position paper of the Society for Adolescent Medicine. *Journal Adolescent Health, 14*, 570–576.

Bolton, B. & Roessler, R. (2008). *Work personality profile*. Hot Springs, AR: National Center on Employment and Disbility.

Borden, B. (2011). *Pictorial inventory of careers (PIC) path-finder*. Jacksonville, FL: Talent Assessment, Inc. Retrieved from http://www.talentassessment.com/pages/PIC

Bowe, F. (2000). *Universal design in education: Teaching nontraditional students*. Westport, CT: Bergin & Garvey.

Brigance, A.H. (1994). *Brigance diagnostic life skills inventory*. North Billerica, MA: Curriculum Associates.

Briggs, K.C., Myers, I.B., McCaulley, M.H., Quenk, N.L., & Hammer, A.L. (1998). *Myers-Briggs Type Indicator*. Mountain View, CA: CPP, Inc.

Bruininks, R.H., Woodcock, R.W., Weatherman, R.F., & Hill, B.K. (1997). *Scales of independent behavior–revised*. Rolling Meadows, IL: Riverside Publishing Co.

Buswell, B., & Sax, C.L. (2002). The three C's of family involvement: Things I wish I had known. In C.L. Sax & C.A. Thoma (Eds.), *Transition assessment: Wise practices for quality lives* (pp. 39–50). Baltimore, MD: Paul H. Brookes Publishing Co.

Cameto, R., Levine, P., & Wagner, M. (2004). *Transition planning for students with disabilities: A special topic report from the National Longitudinal Transition Study-2 (NLTS-2)*. Menlo Park, CA: SRI International.

CAST. (2007). *Principles of universal design*. Retrieved from http://www.cast.org/publications/UDLguidelines/ version1.html.

CAST. (2011). *Universal design for learning guidelines version 2.0*. Wakefield, MA: Author. Retrieved from http:// www.udlcenter.org/aboutudl/udlguidelines

CEC. (2012). *Life-centered education*. Alexandria, VA: Author.

Centers for Disease Control and Prevention. Retrieved from http://www.cdc.gov.

Clark, G.M. (2007). *Assessment for transition planning* (2nd ed.). Austin, TX: PRO-ED.

Cobb, R.B., & Alwell, M. (2009). Transition planning/coordinating interventions for youth with disabilities: A systematic review. *Career Development for Exceptional Individuals, 32*(2), 70–81.

Connecticut Association on Higher Education and Disability (AHEAD) (2008). *Disability documentation guidelines to determine eligibility for accommodations at the postsecondary level.* New London, CT: Author. Retrieved from http://www.ahead.org/aff/ctahead/docguidelines.htm#III

Connecticut State Department of Education. (2009). *2009 guidelines for identifying children with learning disabilities: Executive summary.* Hartford, CT: Author. Retrieved from http://www.ahead.org/laff/ctahead/docguidlines.htm

Connecticut Transition Task Force, Connecticut State Department of Education. (2008). *Transition assessment resource manual.* Hartford, CT: Author.

Conner, J., Pope, D., & Galloway, M. (2010). Success with less stress. *Educational Leadership, 67*(4), 54–58.

Crane, K., & Mooney, M. (2005). *Essential tools: Community resource mapping.* Retrieved from http://www.ncset.org/publications/essentialtools/mapping/default.asp

Curriculum Associates. (2010). *Brigance transition skills inventory.* North Billerica, MA: Author.

Daniels, V.I. (1999). The assessment maze: Making instructional decisions about alternative assessment for students with disabilities. *Preventing School Failure, 43*(4), 171–178.

Davidsen, D.B., & Streagle, K.D. (2011). Developing the transition curriculum. In P. Wehman (Ed.), *Essentials of transition planning* (pp. 41–74). Baltimore, MD: Paul H. Brookes Publishing Co.

Davis, H., Rennick, J., & Majnemer, A. (2011). Transition from pediatric to adult health care for young adults with neurological disorders: Parental perspectives. *Canadian Journal of Neuroscience Nursing, 33*(2), 32–39.

Duke, N.N., & Scal, P.B. (2011). Adult care transitioning for adolescents with special health care needs: A pivotal role for family centered care. *Maternal Child Health Journal, 15*, 98–105.

Dukes, L.L., III. (2010). Gathering data to determine eligibility for services and accommodations. In S.F. Shaw, J.W. Madaus, & L.L. Dukes III (Eds.), *Preparing students with disabilities for college success: A practical guide to transition planning.* Baltimore, MD: Paul H. Brookes Publishing Co.

Dukes, L.L., III, Shaw, S.F., & Madaus, J.W. (2007). How to complete a summary of performance for students exiting to postsecondary education. *Assessment for Effective Intervention, 32*, 143–159.

Dunning, D., Heath, C., & Suls, J.M. (2005). Flawed self-assessment: Implications for health, education and the workplace. *Psychological Science in the Public Interest, 5*(3), 69–106.

Educational Testing Services (2007). Digital Transformation: A Framework for ICT Literacy. Retrieved from http://www.ets.org/Media/Tests/Information_and_Communication_Technology_Literacy/ictreport.pdf

Elliott, S.N., & Roach, A.T. (2007). Alternate assessments of students with significant disabilities: Alternative approaches, common technical challenges. *Applied Measurement in Education, 20*(3), 301–333.

Enderle, J., & Severson, S. (2003). *Enderlee-Severson transition rating scales* (3rd ed.). Morehead, MN: ESTR Publications.

Field, S. & Hoffman, A. (2005). *Steps to Self-Determination,* 2nd ed. Austin, TX: ProEd.

Ford, A., Schnoor, R., Meyer, L., Davern, L., Black, J., & Dempsey, P. (1989). *The Syracuse community referenced guide for students with moderate and severe disabilities* (pp. 377–378). Baltimore, MD: Paul H. Brookes Publishing.

Forest, M., & Pearpoint, J.C. (1992). Putting all kids on the MAP. *Educational Leadership, 50*, 26–31.

Frist, M.B., Fraces, A., & Pincus, H.A. (2002). *DSM-IV-TR Handbook of Differential Diagnosis.* Arlington, VA: American Psychiatric Publishing, Inc.

Gaumer Erickson, A., Clark, G.M., & Patton J.R. (2013). *Informal assessments for transition planning, Second Edition.* Austin TX: PRO-ED.

Geenen, S., Powers, L., Lopez-Vasquez, A., & Bersani, H. (2003). Understanding and promoting the transition of minority adolescents. *Career Development for Exceptional Individuals, 26*, 27–46.

Geenen, S.J., Powers, L.E., & Sells, W. (2003). Understanding the role of health care providers during the transition of adolescents with disabilities and special health care needs. *Society for Adolescent Medicine, 32*, 225–223.

Getzel, E.E., Deschamps, A., & Thoma, C.A. (2010). Transition individualized education planning and summary of performance. In C.A. Thoma & P. Wehman, *Making the most out of IEPs: An educator's guide to the student-directed approach* (pp. 173–188). Baltimore, MD: Paul H. Brookes Publishing Co.

Giangreco, M.F., Cloninger, C.J., & Iverson, V.S. (2011). *Choosing outcomes and accommodations for children: A guide to educational planning for students with disabilities* (3rd. ed.). Baltimore, MD: Paul H. Brookes Publishing Co.

Glutting, J.J. & Wilkinson, G.S. (2003). Wide range interest and occupational test, 2nd ed. San Antonio, TX: Pearson.

Greene, G. (2011). *Transition planning for culturally and linguistically diverse youth.* Baltimore, MD: Paul H. Brookes Publishing Co.

Grigal, M., & Deschamps, A. (2012). Transition education for adolescents with intellectual disabilities. In M.L. Wehmeyer & K.W. Webb (Eds.), *Handbook of adolescent transition education for youth with disabilities* (pp. 398–416). New York, NY: Routledge.

Halpern, A.S., Herr, C.M., Wolf, N.K., Doren, B., Johnson, M.D., & Lawson, J.D. (2000). *Next S.T.E.P.: Student transition and educational planning* (2nd ed.). Austin, TX: PRO-ED.

Hanley-Maxwell, C., Pogoloff, S. M., & Whitney-Thomas, J. (1998). Families: The heart of transition. In F. Rusch & J. Chadsey (Eds.). *Beyond high school: Transition from school to work* (pp. 234–264). Belmont, CA: Wadsworth.

Harrison, P.L. & Oakland, T. (2003). *The adaptive behavior assessment system* (2nd ed.) Torrence, CA: Western Psychological Services.

Health Care Transition Center. *Health care transition transfer of care check list (young adult).* Retrieved from http://www.gottransition.org/UploadedFiles/Files/5.3_HCT_Transfer_Checklist_-_Adult.pdf

Henderson, C. (1999). *College freshmen with disabilities: Statistical year 1998.* Washington, DC: American Council on Education.

Here are the facts. (2011). Retrieved July 8, 2012, from http://www.actionforhealthykids.org/who-we-are/facts

Hoffman, A., Field, S., & Sawilowsky, S. (2004). *Self-determination assessment: Battery user's guide* (3rd ed.). Detroit, MI: Center for Self-Determination and Transition, College of Education, Wayne State University.

Holburn, S., Gordon, A., & Vietze, P.M. (2007). *Person-centered planning made easy: The PICTURE method.* Baltimore, MD: Paul H. Brookes Publishing Co.

Hoover, J. J., & Patton, J. R. (2007). *Curriculum adaptations for students with learning and behavior problems: Principles and practices* (3rd ed.). Austin, TX: PRO-ED.

Hughes, C., & Carter, E.W. (2002). Informal assessment procedures. In C.L. Sax & C.A. Thoma, *Transition assessment: Wise practices for quality lives.* Baltimore, MD: Paul H. Brookes Publishing Co.

Hughes, C., & Carter, E.W. (2000). *The transition handbook: Strategies high school teachers use that work!* Baltimore, MD: Paul H. Brookes Publishing Co.

Hughes, C., & Carter, E.W. (2012). *The new transition handbook: Strategies secondary high school teachers use that work!* Baltimore, MD: Paul H. Brookes Publishing Co.

Hughes, C., Pitkin, S.E., & Lorden, S.W. (1998). Assessing preferences and choices of persons with severe and profound disabilities. *Education and Training in Mental Retardation and Developmental Disabilities, 33,* 299–316.

Idaho Department of Health and Welfare. (2010). *Your future your life.* Retrieved from http://hctransitions.ichp.ufl.edu/pdfs/HCT_Workbook_18up.pdf

Individuals with Disabilities Education Improvement Act (IDEA) of 2004. PL 108-446, 20 U.S.C. §§ 1400 et seq.

Individuals with Disabilities Education Act of 2004. 20 U. S. C. § 1400 et seq. (2004).

Job Accommodation Network. Retrieved from http://askjan.org/topics/forms.htm.

Jordan, M. (2008). Supporting individuals with autism spectrum disorders: Quality employment practices. *The Institute Brief, 25,* Boston, MA: Institute for Community Inclusion.

Kallio, A., & Owens, L. (2007). *Opening doors to postsecondary education: Planning for life after high school: A handbook for students, school counselors, teachers, parents.* Madison, WI: Wisconsin Department of Public Instruction. Retrieved October 15, 2011, from http://dpi.wi.gov/sped/transition.html

Karvonen, M., & Huynh, H. (2007). Relationship between IEP characteristics and test scores on an alternate assessment for students with significant cognitive disabilities. *Applied Measurement in Education, 20*(3), 273–300.

Kaufman, A.S., & Kaufman, N.L. (2004) Kaufman test of educational achievement, 2nd ed. San Antonio, TX: Pearson.

Kendall, J.S., Pollack, C., Schwols, A., & Snyder, C. (2007, June). High school standards and expectations for college and the workplace. *Issues and Answers Report, REL 2007-no. 001.* Washington, DC: U.S. Department of Education, Institute of Education Sciences, National Center for Education Evaluation and Regional Assistance, Regional Educational Laboratory Central. Retrieved from http://ies.ed.gov/ncee/edlabs/regions/central/pdf/REL_2007001_sum.pdf

Kennedy, A., Sloman, F., Douglass, J.A., & Sawyer, S.M. (2007). Young people with chronic illness: The approach to transition. *Internal Medicine Journal,* 37, 555–560.

Keyes, M.W., & Owens-Johnson, L. (2003). Developing person-centered IEPs. *Intervention in School and Clinic, 38*(3), 145–152.

Kim, K.H., & Morningstar, M.E. (2005). Transition planning involving culturally and linguistically diverse families. *Career Development for Exceptional Individuals, 28,* 92–103.

Kim, K.H., & Turnbull, A. (2004). Transition to adulthood for students with severe intellectual disabilities: shifting toward person-family interdependent planning. *Research and Practice for Persons with Severe Disabilities, 29*(1), 53–57.

Kleinert, H.L., Garrett, B., Towles, E., Garrett, M., Nowak-Drabik, K., Waddell, C., & Kearns, J.F. (2002). Alternate assessment scores and life outcomes for students with significant disabilities: Are they related? *Assessment for Effective Intervention, 42,* 19. doi:10.1177/073724770202800103

Kober, N., & Rentner, D.S. (2012). *State education agency funding and staffing in the education reform era.* Washington, DC: Center for Education Policy.

Kochhar-Bryant, C., & Bassett, D. (2002). *Aligning transition and standards-based education.* Columbus, OH: Merrill/Prentice Hall.

Kochhar-Bryant, C.A. with Shaw, S., & Izzo, M. (2007). *What every teacher should know about transition and IDEA 2004.* Boston, MA: Pearson.

Knapp, L.F. & Knapp, R.R. (1976). *Career ability placement, survey.* San Diego, CA: Educational and Industrial Testing Service.

Kuder career search with person match. Retrieved from http://www.kuder.com/solutions/kuder-assessments.aspx#kuder_career_search

Landmark College. (2009). *A guide to assessing college readiness for college-bound students with learning disabilities or AD/HD.* Landmark College, Puntey, VT.

Lee, H.J. (2010). *Comparison of perceptions toward person-centered planning (PCP) of secondary educators in the US and Korea.* (Unpublished master's thesis). University of Kansas, Lawrence.

Ma, X. (1999). Dropping out of advanced mathematics: The effects of parental involvement. *Teachers College Record, 101,* 60–81.

Madaus, J.W. (2010). Let's be reasonable: Accommodations at the college level. In S.F. Shaw, J.W. Madaus, & L.L. Dukes III (Eds.), *Preparing students with disabilities for college success: A practical guide to transition planning.* Baltimore, MD: Paul H. Brookes Publishing Co.

Madaus, J.W., Banerjee, M., & Hamblet, E. (2010). Learning disability documentation decision making at the postsecondary level. *Career Development for Exceptional Individuals, 33*(2), 68–79.

Markwardt, F.C. (1997). *Peabody individual achievement test-revised.* San Antonio, TX: Pearson.

Martin, J.E., Hennessey, M.N., McConnell, A.E., Terry, R.A., Kazimi, N.A., Willis, D.M., & Martin, J.D. (2012). *Transition assessment and goal generator.* Norman, OK: University of Oklahoma's Zarrow Center.

Martin, J.E., Huber-Marshall, L.H., Maxson, L., Jerman, P., Hughes, W., Miller, T., & McGill, T. (2000). *Choice maker set: Tools for school-to-work transition.* Frederick, CO: Sopris West.

Martin, J.E., Marshall, L.H., & DePry, R.L. (2008). Participatory decision-making: Innovative practices that increase student self-determination. In R.W. Flexer, T.J. Simmons, P. Luft, & R.M. Baer (Eds.), *Transition planning for secondary students with disabilities* (3rd ed.). Columbus, OH: Merrill Prentice Hall.

Martin, J.E, Huber-Marshall, L.H., Wray, D., O'Brien, J., Wells, L., Olvey, G.H., Johnson, Z., Jerman, P., & Maxon, L. (2007). *Choicemaker self-determination transition curriculum* (2nd ed.). Longmont, CO: Sopris West.

Martin, J.E., Marshall, L.H., Maxson, L.M., & Jerman, P.L. (1996). *The self-directed IEP*. Longmont, CO: Sopris West.

Martin, J.E., Van Dycke, J.L., Greene, B.A., Gardner, J.E., Christensen, W.R., Woods, I.L., et al. (2006). Direct observation of teacher-directed IEP meetings: Establishing the need for student IEP meeting instruction. *Exceptional Children, 72*, 187–200.

Martin, J.E., Zhang, D.D., & Test, D. (2012). Student involvement in the transition process. In M.L. Wehmeyer & K.W. Webb (Eds.), *Handbook of transition for youth with disabilities* (pp. 56–72). New York, NY: Routledge, Taylor, & Francis.

Martorell, A., Gutierrez-Recacha, P., Perda, A., & Ayuso-Mateos, J.L. (2008). Identification of personal factors that determine work outcome for adults with intellectual disability. *Journal of Intellectual Disability Research, 52*(12), 1091–1101.

Mason, C., McGahee-Kovac, M., Johnson, L., & Stillerman, S. (2002). Implementing student-led IEPs: Student participation and student and teacher reactions. *Career Development for Exceptional Individuals, 25*, 171–192.

Maynard, J., De Sousa, M., Needham, J., Smith, F., McDonagh, J.E. (2004). *Adolescent transition care: Guidance for nursing staff*. Royal College of Nursing, London, U.K.

McGuire, J.M. (2010). Considerations for the transition to college. In S.F. Shaw, J.W. Madaus, and L.C. Dukes (Eds.). *Preparing students with disabilities for college success: A practical guide to transition planning*. Baltimore, MD: Paul H. Brookes Publishing Company.

Mesibov, G., Thomas, J.B., Chapman, S.M., & Schopler, E. (2007). *TEACCH transition assessment profile* (2nd ed.). Austin, TX: PRO-ED.

Miller, R.J. Lombard, R.C., & Corbey, S.A. (2007). Transition assessment: Planning transition and IEP development for youth with mild to moderate disabilities. Boston, MA: Pearson.

Mittal, S.K., Ahern, L., Flaster, E., Maesaka, J.K., & Fishbane, S. (2001). Self assessed physical and mental function of haemodialysis patients. *Nephrol Dial Transplant, 16*, 1387–1394.

Morningstar, M.E. (2008). *Transition assessment: The big picture*. Retrieved from http://transitioncoalition.org/transition/module_home.php

Morningstar, M.E., & Liss, J.M. (2008). A preliminary investigation of how states are responding to the transition assessment requirements under IDEIA 2004. *Career development for exceptional individuals, 31*, 48–55.

Morningstar, M.E., Wehmeyer, M.L., & Dove, S.D. (2008). The role of families in enhancing transition outcomes for youth with learning disabilities. In G. Blalock, J. Patton, & P. Kohler (Eds.), *Transition and student with learning disabilities: Facilitating the movement from school to adult life* (2nd ed., pp. 79–103). Austin, TX: PRO-ED

Mount, B. (2000). *Person-centered planning: Finding directions for change using personal futures planning*. New York, NY: Capacity Institute.

Myers, I.B., & McCaulley, M.H. (1985). *Manual: A guide to the development and use of the Myers-Briggs Type Indicator*. Palo Alto, CA: Consulting Psychologists Press.

National Association of State Directors of Career Technical Education Consortium. Student interest survey for career clusters. Retrieved from http://www.tstc.edu/pyp

National Center for Education Statistics. (2011, April). Postsecondary education. *Digest of Education Statistics: 2010*. Retrieved from http://nces.ed.gov/programs/digest/d10/ch_3.asp

National Center on Secondary Education and Transition. (2005). *Essential tools: Improving secondary education and transition for youth with disabilities, community resource mapping*. Washington, DC: U.S. Department of Education, Office of Special Education Programs.

National Center on Workforce and Disability. Career Exploration. Retrieved June 29, 2012, http://www.onestops.info/article.php?article_id=85

Neubert, D. (2012). Transition assessment for adolescents. In M.L. Wehmeyer & K.W. Webb (Eds.), *Handbook of adolescent transition education for youth with disabilities* (pp. 73–90). New York, NY: Routledge.

Newman, L., Wagner, M., Cameto, R., & Knokey, A.M. (2009). *The post–high school outcomes of youth with disabilities up to 4 years after high school: A report of findings from the National Longitudinal Transition Study-2 (NLTS2)* (NCSER 2009–3017). Retrieved from http://www.nlts2.org/reports/2009_04/nlts2_report_2009_04_complete.pdf

Nota, L., Ferrari, L., Soresi, S., & Wehmeyer, M.L. (2007). Self-determination, social abilities, and the quality of life of people with intellectual disabilities. *Journal of Intellectual Disability Research, 51*, 850-865.

O'Brien, J., & Callahan, M. (2010). Employment support as knowledge creation. *Research and Practice for Persons with Severe Disabilities, 27*(3), 173–176.

Office of Disability Employment Policy, U.S. Department of Labor . Skills to pay the bills: Mastering soft skills for workplace success. Retrieved from http://www.dol.gov/odep/

Orkwis, R., & McLane, K. (1998). A curriculum every student can use: Design principles for student access. ERIC/OSEP Topical Brief. Reston, VA: ERIC/OSEP Special Project.

Pankaskie, S.C., & Chandler, S.K. (2012). Social skills. In J. Kregel & P. Wehman (Eds.), *Functional curriculum for elementary and secondary students with special needs* (pp. 285–317). Austin, TX: PRO-ED.

Parker, R.M. (2002). *Occupational Aptitude Survey and Interest Schedule* (3rd Ed.). Austin, TX: ProEd.

Patrikakou, E.N. (1996). Investigating the academic achievement of adolescents with learning disabilities: A structural modeling approach. *Journal of Educational Psychology, 88*, 435–450.

Patton, J.R., & Clark, G.M. (In press). *Transition Planning Inventory, Second Edition*. Austin, TX: PRO-ED.

Pearpoint, J.C., O'Brien, J., & Forest, M. (1993). *PATH: Planning possible, positive futures*. Toronto, Canada: Inclusion Press.

Portley, J.L., Martin, J.E., & Hennessey, M.N. (2012). *Examination of high school transition program variables associated with successful student outcomes.* (Manuscript submitted for publication).

The Post-High School Outcomes of Young Adults With Disabilities up to 8 Years After High School: A Report From the National Longitudinal Transition Study-2 (NLTS2) September 2011. Retrieved from http://www.nlts2.org/reports/2011_09_02/nlts2_report_2011_09_02_execsum.pdf on June 30, 2012

Pywell, A. (2010). Transition: Moving on well from pediatric to adult health care. *British Journal of Nursing, 19*(10), 652–656.

Rapley, P., & Davidson, P.M. (2009). Enough of the problem: A review of the time for health care transition solutions for young adults with chronic illness. *Journal of Clinical Nursing, 19,* 313–323.

Raue, K., and Lewis, L. (2011). *Students with disabilities at degree-granting postsecondary institutions* (NCES 2011–018). U.S. Department of Education, National Center for Education Statistics. Washington, DC: U.S. Government Printing Office.

Reiss, J., & Gibson, R. (2005). Health Care Transition Workbook. Retrieved from http://www.doh.state.fl.us/alternate sites/cms-kids/kids_teens/documents/trans_workbook _15-17.pdf

Reiss, J., & Gibson, R. (2005). Health Care Transition Planning Guide for Youth and Families: Ages 18 and Older. Gainesville, FL: Institute for Child Health Policy. Retrieved from http://hctransitions.ichp.edu/products _planning_guides.php

Repetto, J.B., Gibson, R.W., Lubbers, J., Gritz, S., & Reiss, J. (2008). A statewide study of knowledge and attitudes regarding health care transition. *Career Development for Exceptional Individuals, 31*(1), 5–13.

Rice, C. (2008). *Tools for transition.* Dahlonega, GA: Piney Mountain Press.

Roeber, E. (2002). *Setting standards on alternate assessments* (Synthesis Report 42). Minneapolis, MN: University of Minnesota, National Center on Educational Outcomes. Retrieved from http://education.umn.edu/NCEO/Online Pubs/Synthesis42.html

Rojewski, J.W. (2002). Career assessment for adolescents with mild disabilities: Critical concerns for transition planning. *Career Development for Exceptional Individuals, 25,* 73–95.

Rosenburg, H., & Brady, M.P. (2000). *Job observation and behavior scales.* Wood Dale, IL: Stoelting Co.

Satcher, D. (2010). Taking charge of school wellness. *Educational Leadership, 67*(4), 38–43.

Schwartz, L.A., Tuchman, L.K., Hobbie, W.L., & Ginsberg, J.P. (2011). A socio-ecological model of readiness for transition to adult oriented care for adolescents and young adults with chronic health conditions. *Child: Care, Health and Development, 37*(6), 883–895.

Scott, L.A., Saddler, S., Thoma, C.A., Bartholomew, C., Alder, N., & Tamura, R. (2011). Universal design for transition: A multi-element brief experimental single subject design study of the impact of the use of UDT on student achievement, engagement and motivation. *i-manager's Journal on Educational Psychology, 4*(4), 21–32.

Shaw, S.F., Dukes, L.L., III, & Madaus, J.W. (2012, May/June). Beyond compliance: Using the summary of performance to enhance transition planning. *Teaching Exceptional Children, 44*(5), 6–12.

Shogren, K.A. (2011). Culture and self-determination: A synthesis of the literature and directions for future research and practice. *Career Development for Exceptional Individuals, 34,* 115–127.

Shogren, K.A., Lopez, S.J., Wehmeyer, M.L., Little, T.D., & Pressgrove, C.L. (2006). The role of positive psychology constructs in predicting life satisfaction in adolescents with and without cognitive disabilities: An exploratory study. *The Journal of Positive Psychology, 1,* 37–52.

Sitlington, P.L. (2008). Students with reading and writing challenges: Using informal assessment to assist in planning for the transition to adult life. *Reading and Writing Quarterly, 24,* 77–100.

Sitlington, P.L., Neubert, D.A., Begun, W.H., Lombard, R.C., & Leconte, P.J. (2007). *Assess for success: A practitioner's handbook on transition assessment* (2nd ed.). Thousand Oaks, CA: Corwin Press.

Sitlington, P., Neubert, D., & Clark, G. (2010). *Transition education and services for adolescents with disabilities* (5th ed.). Boston, MA: Pearson: Allyn & Bacon.

Sitlington, P.L., Neubert, D.A., & Leconte, P.J. (1997). Transition assessment: The position of the Division on Career Development and Transition. *Career Development for Exceptional Individuals, 20,* 69–79.

Sparrow, S.S., Cicchetti, D.V., & Balla, D.A. (2005). *Vineland adaptive behavior scales* (2nd ed.). Circle Pines, MN: American Guidance Services.

Spinelli, C.G. (2012). *Classroom assessment for students in special and general education* (3rd ed.). Boston, MA: Pearson.

Synatuschk, K.O., Clark, G.M., Patton, J.R., & Copeland, L.R. (2007). *Informal assessments for transition: Employment and career planning.* Austin, TX: PRO-ED.

Test, D.W. (2012). *Evidence-based instructional strategies for transition.* Baltimore, MD: Paul H. Brookes Publishing Co.

Test, D.W., Aspel, N.P., & Everson, J.M. (2006). *Transition Methods for Youth with Disabilities.* Upper Saddle River, NJ: Pearson Merrill Prentice Hall.

Test, D.W., Mason, C., Hughes, C., Konrad, M., Neale, M., & Wood, W. (2004). Student involvement in individualized education program meetings. *Exceptional Children, 57*(1), 6–14.

Thoma, C.A., Bartholomew, C.C., & Scott, L.A. (2009). *Universal design for transition: A roadmap for planning and instruction.* Baltimore, MD: Paul H. Brookes Publishing Co.

Thoma, C.A., Bartholomew, C.C., Tamura, R., Scott, L.A., & Terpstra, J. E. (2008). *UDT: Applying a universal design approach to link transition and academics.* Preconference workshop at the Council for Exceptional Children Convention, Boston, MA.

Thoma, C.A., Boyd, K., & Austin, K. (2013). Assessment and teaching for transition. In P. Wehman, *Life beyond the classroom* (5th ed., pp. 235–260). Baltimore, MD: Paul H. Brookes Publishing Co.

Thoma, C.A., & Getzel, E.E. (2005). Self-determination is what it's all about: What post-secondary students with disabilities tell us are important considerations for success. *Education and Training in Mental Retardation and Developmental Disabilities, 40,* 35–48.

Thoma, C.A., & Held, M.A. (2002). Measuring what's important: Using alternative assessments. In C. Sax & C.A. Thoma (Eds.), *Transition assessment: Wise practices for quality lives* (pp. 71–85). Baltimore, MD: Paul H. Brookes Publishing Co.

Thoma, C.A., & Held, M.F. (2003). Strategies for supporting self-determination of high school students with disabilities: What can be done after the meeting. Presentation at Division on Developmental Disabilities Conference, Kauai, HI.

Thoma, C.A., Saddler, S., Purvis, B., & Scott, L.A. (2010). Essentials of the student-directed IEP process. In C.A. Thoma & P. Wehman (Eds.), *Getting the most out of IEPs: An educator's guide to the student-directed approach* (pp. 1–23). Baltimore, MD: Paul H. Brookes Publishing Co.

Thoma, C.A., & Wehman, P. (2010). *Getting the most out of IEPs: An educator's guide to the student-directed approach.* Baltimore, MD: Paul H. Brookes Publishing Co.

Thompson, J.R., Bryant, B., Campbell, E.M., Craig, E.M., Hughes, C., Rotholz, D.A., et al. (2004). *Supports Intensity Scale (SIS)*. Washington, DC: American Association on Mental Retardation.

Thompson, J.R., Fulk B.M., & Piercy, S.W. (2001). Do individualized transition plans match the postschool projections of students with learning disabilities and their parents? *Career Development for Exceptional Individuals, 23*, 3–25.

Tilson, G. (n.d.). [Developing a positive profile. Retrieved from http://www.thinkcollege.net/for-professionals/assessment-tools]; adapted by permission.

Torgerson, C. W., Miner, C. A., & Shen, H. (2004). Developing student competence in self-directed IEPs. *Intervention in School and Clinic, 39*, 162–167.

Trainor, A.A. (2008). Using cultural and social capital to improve postsecondary outcomes and expand transition models for youth with disabilities. *The Journal of Special Education, 42*, 148–163.

Uphold, N.M., Walker, A.R., & West, D.W. (2007). Resources for involving students in their IEP process. *TEACHING Exceptional Children Plus, 3*(4), Article 1. Retrieved November 7, 2012 from http://escholarship.bc.edu/education/tecplus/vol3/iss4/art1

U.S. Department of Education. (2005). *Alternate achievement standards for students with the most significant cognitive disabilities: Non-regulatory guidance.* Washington, DC: U.S. Department of Education, Office of Elementary and Secondary Education.

U.S. Department of Education. (2007). Students with disabilities preparing for postsecondary education: Know your rights and responsibilities. Washington, DC: U.S. Government Printing Office.

U.S. Department of Education, National Center for Education Statistics (2011). Fast Facts. Retrieved February 28, 2012 from http://nces.ed.gov/fastfacts/display.asp?id=60.

U.S. Department of Labor. (2002) http://www.onetcenter.org/IP.html?p=2 Retrieved from on July 1, 2012

U.S. Military Entrance Processing Command. (2005). *Armed services vocational aptitude battery* [Forms 18/19]. North Chicago, IL: Author

Van Reusen, A.K., Bos, C.S., Schumaker, J.B., & Deshler, D.D. (1994). *The self advocacy strategy: Transition skills list.* Lawrence, KS: Edge Enterprises.

Venn, J.J. (2000). *Assessing students with special needs* (2nd ed.). Upper Saddle River, NJ: Merrill.

Virginia Department of Education. (2010). Secondary Transition: Why it's important to plan early. Retrieved January 19, 2012, from http://www.doe.virginia.gov/special_ed/regulations/state/fast_facts/fast_fact_secondary_transition.pdf

Virginia Department of Health, Partnership for People with Disabilities. (2010). Health care disparities focus groups: The experience of Latino and African American parents of children with disabilities and special health care needs. Retrieved from http://www.partnership.vcu.edu/documents/Final_Health_Care_Disparities_Report.pdf

Wagner, M., Newman, L., Cameto, R., Levine, P., & Marder, C. (2007). Perceptions and expectations of youth with disabilities: A special topic report from the National Longitudinal Transition Study–2 (NLTS-2). Menlo Park, CA: SRI International. Retrieved from http://www.nlts2.org/reports/2007_08/nlts2_report_2007_08_complete.pdf

Wandry, D.L., & Pleet, A.M. (2012). Family involvement in transition planning. In M.L. Wehmeyer & K.W. Webb (Eds.), *Handbook of adolescent transition education for youth with disabilities* (pp. 102–118). New York, NY: Routledge.

Watson, A.R. (2000). Non-compliance and transfer from pediatric to adult transplant unit. *Pediatric Nephrology, 14*(6), 469–472.

Wehman, P., & Brooke, V. (2013). Securing meaningful work in the community: vocational internships, placements, and careers. In P. Wehman, *Life beyond the classroom* (5th ed., pp. 309–338). Baltimore, MD: Paul H. Brookes Publishing Co.

Wehman, P., & Kregel, J. (2012). *Functional Curriculum for Elementary and Secondary Students with Special Needs.* Austin, TX: PRO-ED

Wehman, P., Smith, M.D., & Schall, C. (2009). *Autism & the transition to adulthood: Success beyond the classroom.* Baltimore, MD: Paul H. Brookes Publishing Co.

Wehmeyer, M.L. (2006). Self-determination and individuals with severe disabilities: Reexamining meanings and misconceptions. *Research and Practice in Severe Disabilities, 30*, 113–120.

Wehmeyer, M.L., Agran, M., & Hughes, C. (1998). *Teaching self-determination to students with disabilities: Basic skills for successful transition* (pp. 104–107). Baltimore, MD: Paul H. Brookes Publishing Co.

Wehmeyer, M.L., Agran, M., Hughes, C., Martin, J., Mithaug, D.E., & Palmer, S. (2007). *Promoting self-determination in students with intellectual and developmental disabilities.* New York, NY: Guilford Press.

Wehmeyer, M.L., & Field, S.L. (2007). *Self-determination: Instructional and assessment strategies.* Thousand Oaks, CA: Corwin Press.

Wehmeyer, M.L., Field, S.L., & Thoma, C.A. (2012). Self-determination and adolescent transition education. In M.L. Wehmeyer & K.W. Webb (Eds.), *Handbook of adolescent transition education for youth with disabilities* (pp. 171–190). New York, NY: Routledge.

Wehmeyer, M.L., & Kelchner, K. (1995a). *The ARC's self-determination scale.* Arlington, TX: ARC National Headquarters.

Wehmeyer, M.L., & Kelchner, K. (1995b). *The ARC's self-determination scale: Procedural guidelines.* Arlington, TX: Author.

Wehmeyer, M.L., Lawrence, M., Kelchner, K., Palmer, S., Garner, N., & Soukup, J. (2004). *Whose future is it anyway? A student-directed transition planning process* (2nd ed.). Lawrence, KS: Beach Center on Disability.

Wehmeyer, M.L., Morningstar, M.E., & Husted, D. (1999). *Family involvement in transition planning and program implementation.* Austin, TX: PRO-ED.

Wehmeyer, M.L., & Palmer, S.B. (2003). Adult outcomes from students with cognitive disabilities three years after high school. *Education and Training in Developmental Disabilities, 38,* 131–144.

Wehmeyer, M.L., & Palmer, S.B. (2011). *Whose future is it?* Verona, WI: Attainment Company.

Wehmeyer, M.L., & Schwartz, M. (1997). Self-determination and positive adult outcomes: A follow up study of youth with mental retardation or learning disabilities. *Exceptional Children, 63,* 245–255.

Wehmeyer, M.L., & Shogren, K.A. (2013). Self-determination: Getting students involved in leadership. In Wehman, P., *Life beyond the classroom: Transition strategies for young people with disabilities* (5th ed., pp. 41–68). Baltimore, MD: Paul H. Brookes Publishing Co.

While, A., Forbes, A., Ullman, R., Lewis, S., Mathes, L., & Griffiths, P. (2004). Good practices that address continuity during transition from child to adult care: Synthesis of the evidence. *Child Care Health Development, 30*(5), 439–452.

Wiggins, G., & McTighe, J. (2006). *Understanding by design* (expanded 2nd ed.). Upper Saddle River, NJ: Pearson Education.

Wiggins, G., & McTighe, J. (2011). The understanding by design guide to creating high-quality units. Alexandria, VA: Association for Supervision and Curriculum Development (ASCD).

Wiktionary. (2012). Assidere definition. Retrieved October 2012 from http://en.wiktionary.org/wiki/assidere

Williams, T. (2008). *Transition planning for culturally and linguistically diverse (CLD) families of youth with disabilities: Issues and trends.* Tracey Williams University of Kansas. Retrieved from http://transitioncoalition.org/transition/tcfiles/files/docs/CLD_Summer_Institute _08ppt1262564762.pps/CLD_Summer_Institute_08ppt .pps

Woodcock, R.W., McGrew, K.S., & Mather, N. (2007). *Woodcock-Johnson NU III tests of achievement.* Itasca, IL: Riverside.Zarrow Center (n.d.). Mission of the Zarrow Center. Retrieved from http://www.ou.edu/content/education/centers-and-partnerships/zarrow.html

Appendix

List of Transition Assessments

Transition Assessment Chart

Title	Academic	Self-determination	Employment	Postsecondary	Health	Community leisure recreation	Social skills	Publisher/ website	Assessment type	CD-ROM?	Web-based?
AAIDD Diagnostic Adaptive Behavior Scale (DABS)	x	x	x				x	AAIDD http://www.aaidd.org	NR		
AAIDD Supports Intensity Scale (SIS)	x		x	x		x	x	AAIDD http://www.siswebsite.org	NR		x
Ability Explorer (AE)			x					JIST Publishing http://www.jist.com	CR		
AccuVision Workplace Success Skills (WSS)		x	x				x	The Resource Connection http://www.resourceconnection.com	O		
ACT	x							ACT, Inc. http://www.act.org	NR		x
Adaptive Behavior Evaluation Scale, Revised–Second Edition (ABES-R2)	x	x			x	x	x	Hawthorne Educational Services http://hawthorne-ed.com/	NR	x	x
Adaptive Behavior Inventory (ABI)						x	x	PRO-ED, Inc http://www.proedinc.com	NR		
Adult Personality Inventory		x	x					Institute for Personality and Ability Testing http://www.ipat.com	NR		
AIR Self-Determination Scale		x					x	Zarrow Center http://www.ou.edu/zarrow/	CR		
Ansell-Casey Life Skills Assessment (ACLSA)	x	x	x		x	x	x	Casey Family Programs http://caseylifeskills.force.com/	CR		x
Arc Self-Determination Scale		x					x	The ARC of the United States http://www.ou.edu/content/dam/Education/documents/miscellaneous/the-arc-self-determination-scale.pdf	CR		
Armed Services Vocational Aptitude Battery (ASVAB)											

Key: NR = norm-referenced; CR = criterion-referenced; C = checklist; O = other

Transition Assessment Chart (continued)

Title	Academic	Self-determination	Employment	Postsecondary	Health	Community leisure recreation	Social skills	Publisher/ website	Assessment type	CD-ROM?	Web-based?
ASVAB–Career and Exploration Program (sample)—online			x					United States Military Entrance Processing Command http://www.official-asvab.com	NR		x
Ashland Interest Assessment			x					Sigma Assessment Systems http://www.sigmaassessmentsystems.com	NR		
Assessing Students' Needs for Assistive Technology–Fifth Edition (ASNAT-5)	x					x	x	WATI http://www.wati.org	O		
Autism Screening Instrument for Educational Planning–Third Edition (ASIEP-3)	x						x	PRO-ED, Inc. http://www.proedinc.com	NR		
Barriers to Employment Success Inventory (BESI)	x		x				x	JIST Publishing http://www.jist.com	CR		
Barsch Learning Style Inventory	x		x	x				Academic Therapy Publications http://www.academictherapy.com	CR		
Becker Work Adjustment Profile–Second Edition (BWAP-2)	x		x				x	PRO-ED, Inc. http://www.proedinc.com	NR		
Behavior and Emotional Rating Scale–Second Edition (BERS-2)							x	PRO-ED, Inc. http://www.proedinc.com	NR		
BRIGANCE Comprehensive Inventory of Basic Skills II (CIBS II)	x					x	x	Curriculum Associates, Inc. http://www.curriculumassociates.com	CR		
BRIGANCE Diagnostic Life Skills Inventory (NOTE: being replaced by BRIGANCE Transition Skills Inventory)		x					x	Zarrow Center http://www.ou.edu/zarrow/			
BRIGANCE Transition Skills Inventory (TSI)	x	x	x	x				Curriculum Associates, Inc. http://www.curriculumassociates.com	CR		x

Key: NR = norm-referenced; CR = criterion-referenced; C = checklist; O = other

Transition Assessment Chart *(continued)*

Title	Academic	Self-determination	Employment	Postsecondary	Health	Community leisure recreation	Social skills	Publisher/ website	Assessment type	CD-ROM?	Web-based?
Campbell Interest and Skill Survey (CISS)			x					Pearson Assessments http://www.pearson assessments.com	NR		x
Career Assessment Inventory (CAI)			x	x				Pearson Assessments http://www.pearson assessments.com	NR		x
Career Exploration Inventory–Third Edition (CEI-3)			x	x		x		JIST Publishing http://www.jist.com	NR		
Career Focus 2000 Interest Inventory (CF2II) (NOTE: Being replaced by the Perfect Career Interest Inventory [PCII])			x	x				Gonyea & Associates, Inc. http://www.iccweb.com	O		
The Career Key			x					Lawrence K. Jones http://www.careerkey .org	O		x
Career Scope v10–Comprehensive Career Assessment			x	x				Vocational Research Institute http://www.vri.org	NR	x	
Choices CD Edition (NOTE: Log-in required)				x				Bridges Transition Company http://www.bridges.com			x
College Survival and Success Scale (CSSS)	x			x			x	JIST Publishing http://www.jist.com	NR		
COPSystem Career Measurement Package • Career Occupational Preference System Interest Inventory (COPS) • Career Ability Placement Survey (CAPS) • Career Orientation & Placement Evaluation Survey (COPES)			x	x				EdITS http://www.edits.net	NR		x
COPS-PIC Interest Inventory			x	x				EdITS http://www.edits.net	NR		
Crawford Small Parts Dexterity Test			x					PsychCorp, Hartcourt Assessment, Inc. http://www.psychCorp .com	NR		

Key: NR = norm-referenced; CR = criterion-referenced; C = checklist; O = other

Transition Assessment Chart *(continued)*

Title	Academic	Self-determination	Employment	Postsecondary	Health	Community leisure recreation	Social skills	Publisher/ website	Assessment type	CD-ROM?	Web-based?
Culture Free Self-Esteem Inventories–Third Edition (CFSEI-3)	x	x				x	x	PRO-ED, Inc. http://www.proedinc .com	NR		
Differential Aptitude Test (DAT)	x		x					Pearson Assessments http://www.pearson assessments.com	NR		
Enderle-Severson Transition Rating Scales–Third Edition (ESTRS-3)			x	x	x		x	ESTR Publications transition@estr.net	CR		
Explorer: The Career Game			x				x	JIST Publishing http://www.jist.com	O		
Functional Independence Skills Handbook (FISH)	x		x				x	PRO-ED, Inc. http://www.proedinc.com	CR		
Functional Skills Screening Inventory (FSSI)			x			x		Functional Resources http://www.winfssi.com	O	x	
Hammill Multiability Achievement Test (HAMAT)	x							PRO-ED, Inc. http://www.proedinc.com	NR		
Harrington-O'Shea Career Decision-Making System Revised (CDM-R)			x	x				Pearson Assessments http://www.pearson assessments.com	NR		x
Health Care Transition Transfer of Care Checklist					x			Got Transition http://www.gottransition .org	C		
Health Care Transition Workbook					x			Institute for Child Health Policy, University of Florida Gainesville, Florida http://hctransitions.ichp .ufl.edu/ddcouncil/ resources/module5/HCT _Workbook_15-17.doc	O		
Health and Wellness 101: The Basic Skills					x			Got Transition http://www.gottransition .org	C		
IDEAS: Interest Determination, Exploration, and Assessment System			x					Pearson Assessments http://www.pearson assessments.com	NR		
Iowa Test of Basic Skills (ITBS)	x							Riverside Publishing Company http://www.riverside publishing.com	NR		

Key: NR = norm-referenced; CR = criterion-referenced; C = checklist; O = other

Transition Assessment Chart *(continued)*

Title	Academic	Self-determination	Employment	Postsecondary	Health	Community leisure recreation	Social skills	Publisher/ website	Assessment type	CD-ROM?	Web-based?
Informal Assessments for Transition: Independent Living and Community Participation		x				x	x	PRO-ED, Inc. http://www.proedinc.com	CR		
Informal Assessments for Transition: Employment and Career Planning			x	x				PRO-ED, Inc. http://www.proedinc.com	CR		
Job Observation and Behavior Scale (JOBS)			x				x	Stoelting Company http://www.stoeltingco.com			
Job Observation and Behavior Scale Opportunity for Self-Determination (JOBS: OSD)		x	x					Stoelting Company http://www.stoeltingco.com	NR		
Kaufman Brief Intelligence Test–Second Edition (KBIT-2)	x							Pearson Assessments http://www.pearson assessments.com	NR		
Keirsey Temperament Sorter-II (KTS-II)	x						x	Keirsey.com http://www.keirsey.com/default.aspx			
Life Centered Education (LCE) Transition Curriculum	x	x	x	x	x	x	x	Council for Exceptional Children http://www.cec.sped.org	CR		x
Microcomputer Evaluation of Careers and Academics (MECA)			x	x				The Conover Company http://www.conover company.com	CR	x	
OASIS-III Aptitude Survey			x	x				PRO-ED, Inc. http://www.proedinc.com	NR		
Occupational Outlook Handbook (OOH)								U.S. Department of Labor http://www.bls.gov/oco/	O		
O*NET (Occupational Information Network) Career Exploration Tools			x	x				Occupational Information Network http://www.onetcenter.org	O		
Parent's Health Care Transition Activities Checklist					x			University of Florida http://hctransitions.ichp.ufl.edu/ddcouncil/resources/module5/HCT_Workbook_15-17.doc	C		

Key: NR = norm-referenced; CR = criterion-referenced; C = checklist; O = other

Transition Assessment Chart *(continued)*

Title	Academic	Self-determination	Employment	Postsecondary	Health	Community leisure recreation	Social skills	Publisher/ website	Assessment type	CD-ROM?	Web-based?
Peabody Individual Achievement Test–Revised/Normative Update (PIAT-R/NU)	x							Pearson Assessments http://www.pearson assessments.com	NR		
Pennsylvania Bi-Manual Dexterity Test			x					PRO-ED, Inc. http://www.proedinc .com	CR		
Pennsylvania Transition Health Care Checklist					x			Pennsylvania Department of Health http://www.dsf.health. state.pa.us/health/lib/ health/familyhealth/ transition_hc_checklist revised3-07.pdf	C		
Perfect Career Interest Inventory (PCII)			x	x				Gonyea & Associates, Inc. http://www.iccweb.com	O		
Pictorial Inventory of Careers (PIC-Pathfinder)			x	x				Talent Assessment, Inc. http://www.talent assessment.com	CR	x	
Picture Interest Career Survey (PICS)			x					JIST Publishing http://www.jist.com	NR		
Practical Assessment Exploration System (PAES)	x		x	x				Talent Assessment, Inc. http://www.talent assessment.com	CR		
Quality of Life Questionnaire (QLQ)					x			MHS, Inc. http://www.mhs.com	NR		
Reading-Free Vocational Interest Inventory: 2 (R-FVII:2)			x					PRO-ED, Inc. http://www.proedinc .com	NR		
Responsibility and Independence Scale for Adolescents (RISA)	x		x			x	x	Riverside Publishing http://www.riverside publishing.com	NR		
SAT	x							College Board http://sat.collegeboard .org/home	NR		x
Scales of Independent Behavior–Revised (SIB-R)	x		x			x	x	Riverside Publishing http://www.riverside publishing.com	NR		

Key: NR = norm-referenced; CR = criterion-referenced; C = checklist; O = other

Transition Assessment Chart *(continued)*

Title	Academic	Self-determination	Employment	Postsecondary	Health	Community leisure recreation	Social skills	Publisher/ website	Assessment type	CD-ROM?	Web-based?
Self-Directed Search—Fourth Edition (SDS-4)			x					Psychology Assessment Resources, Inc. http://www.parinc.com			x
Short Employment Tests—Second Edition			x					Pearson Assessments http://www.pearson assessments.com			
Sixteen Personality Factor Questionnaire—Fifth Edition (16PF-5)			x					IPAT http://www.ipat.com	NR		
Social Skills Rating System (SSRS)							x	Pearson Assessments http://www.pearson assessments.com			
Stanford Achievement Test Series—Tenth Edition (Stanford-10)	x							Pearson Assessments http://www.pearson assessments.com	NR		
STARx Questionnaire					x			Cincinnati Children's Hospital Medical Center http://www.cincinnati childrens.org/workarea/ linkit.aspx?linkidentifier =id&itemid=88031&lib id=87719	O		
Street Survival Skills Questionnaire (SSSQ)			x			x		Pearson Assessments http://www.pearson assessments.com	C		
Talent Assessment Program (TAP)			x				x	Talent Assessment, Inc. http://www.talent assessment.com			
The Interest Indicator			x					Conover Company http://www.conover company.com	CR	x	
The Syracuse Community—Referenced Curriculum Guide; for Students with Moderate and Severe Disabilities	x	x	x	x	x	x	x	Paul H. Brookes Publishing Co. http://brookespublishing .com	CR		
The World of Work and You			x	x				JIST Publishing http://www.jist.com	O		
Tools for Transition • Voc-Ties • Learning Working Styles • Pre-vocational Assessment Screen	x		x					Education Associates, Inc. http://www.education associates.com	CR		

Key: NR = norm-referenced; CR = criterion-referenced; C = checklist; O = other

Transition Assessment Chart *(continued)*

Title	Academic	Self-determination	Employment	Postsecondary	Health	Community leisure recreation	Social skills	Publisher/ website	Assessment type	CD-ROM?	Web-based?
Tools for Transition	x		x					Piney Mountain Publishing http://www.piney mountain.com	CR		
Transition Behavior Scale–Second Edition (TBS-2)			x				x	Hawthorne Educational Services, Inc. http://www.hes-inc.com	NR		
Transition Health Care Checklist: Preparing for Life as an Adult					x			Wisconsin Community of Practice on Transition Practice Group on Health http://www.wsti.org/ documents/Conference %20Handouts%202009/ Session%2015/Health %20Care%20Checklist .pdf	C		
Transition Planning Inventory–2 (TPI-2)	x	x	x	x	x	x	x	PRO-ED, Inc. http://www.proedinc.com	NR		
Transition-to-Work Inventory–Third Edition (TWI-3)			x					JIST Publishing http://www.jist.com	NR		
Vineland Adaptive Behavior Scales–Second Edition (Vineland-II)						x	x	Pearson Assessments http://www.pearson assessments.com	NR		
Vocational Adaptation Rating Scales (VARS)			x				x	Stoelting Company http://www.stoeltingco .com			
Walker-McConnell Scale of Social Competence and School Adjustment							x	Cengage Learning http://www.cengage.com	NR		
Weschler Individual Achievement Test–Third Edition (WIAT-3)	x							Pearson Assessments http://www.pearson assessments.com	NR		
Weschler Intelligence Scale for Children–Fourth Edition (WISC-IV)	x							Pearson Assessments http://www.pearson assessments.com	NR		
Wide Range Interest and Occupation Test (WRIOT-2)			x					Pearson Assessments http://www.pearson assessments.com	NR	x	
Woodcock-Johnson III Normative Update (WJ III)	x							Riverside Publishing http://www.riverside publishing.com	NR		

Key: NR = norm-referenced; CR = criterion-referenced; C = checklist; O = other

Transition Assessment Chart *(continued)*

Title	Academic	Self-determination	Employment	Postsecondary	Health	Community leisure recreation	Social skills	Publisher/ website	Assessment type	CD-ROM?	Web-based?
Wonderlic Basic Skills Test (WBST)	x		x					Wonderlic http://www.wonderlic.com	CR		x
Work Adjustment Scale			x					Hawthorne Educational Services http://www.hes-inc.com	CR		
Your Employment Selections (YES!)			x					Technology Research and Innovation in Special Education (TRISPED) Projects http://www.yesjobsearch .com http://www.trisped.org	O		x

Key: NR = norm-referenced; CR = criterion-referenced; C = checklist; O = other

REFERENCES

Clark, G., & Patton, J. (2007). *Assessment for transitions planning* (2nd ed., pp. 87–91). Austin, TX: PRO-ED.

Connecticut Special Education Resource Center (CTSERC), Connecticut Transition Task Force. (2008). *Transition assessment resource manual.* Retrieved June 10, 2012 from http://ctserc.org/transition/transition_assessment.pdf?2fa6f942252db2ec6c621fe255459617=29c8f5028bd67b4100bc9f998294ce49

Morningstar, M.E., & Pearson, M. (2009). *Transition assessments for students with significant disabilities.* Lawrence, KS: University of Kansas, Transition Coalition.

National Secondary Transition Technical Assistance Center (NSTTAC). (2008). *Age appropriate transition guide.* Retrieved June 10, 2012 from http://www.nsttac.org/pdf

Sitlington, P., Neubert, D., Begun, W., Lombard, R., & Leconte, P. (2007). *Assess for success* (2nd ed., pp. 130–136). Thousand Oaks, CA: Corwin Press, DCDT.

Virginia Department of Education and Department of Rehabilitative Services. (2005). *Career assessment resource manual.* Richmond, VA: Author.

Index

Tables, figures, and boxes are indicated by *t*, *f*, and *b*, respectively.

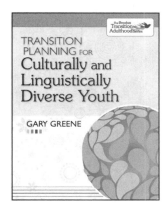